Alfred J. Dull

Green Bay And Fort Howard Directory 1874

Alfred J. Dull

Green Bay And Fort Howard Directory 1874

ISBN/EAN: 9783337731823

Printed in Europe, USA, Canada, Australia, Japan

Cover: Foto ©ninafisch / pixelio.de

More available books at **www.hansebooks.com**

TELULAH MINERAL SPRINGS, *Appleton, Wis.,* HYDE & HARRIMAN, *Proprietors.*

Green Bay and Fort Howard

DIRECTORY.

COMPILED AND ARRANGED BY

J. ALFRED DULL.

CONTAINING

Historical Information of their Early Settlement and Growth; their Present Standing;
Schools, Churches, Societies, etc.

ALSO

BUSINESS DIRECTORY of PRINCIPAL DEALERS.

STREET DIRECTORY, WARD BOUNDARIES, ETC.

APPPETON, WIS.
REID & MILLER, STEAM BOOK AND JOB PRINTERS,
143 & 145 College Avenue,
1874.

DEDICATION.

TO THE

ENTERPRISING

Business and Professional Men,

Who have so kindly encouraged the enterprise, this
work is

Respectfully Dedicated

BY THE

PUBLISHER.

INTRODUCTORY.

In presenting the first volume of the GREEN BAY AND FT. HOWARD DIRECTORY, we feel confident in the assertion that it embraces a large amount of information in regard to the cities which cannot but prove interesting and useful to their citizens. Much of it has never before been given to the public, and no labor has been spared to make it as accurate as possible in all its details. The information it contains has been gathered from the most authentic sources available, and while claiming for it a degree of accuracy not always attained in a work of this kind, yet to convey the idea that it is entirely free from errors, would be asserting a proficiency seldom attained.

The DIRECTORY shows a list of about 3,000 names, which multiplied by 4, the usual number, would indicate a population of about 12,000.

To the gentlemen who have so kindly assisted us we return our grateful thanks, and trust our efforts may meet with their cordial approval.

Truly yours,

J. ALFRED DULL.

Green Bay, Nov. 10, 1874.

INDEX.

GREEN BAY.

ADVERTISEMENTS.

FORT HOWARD.

ADVERTISEMENTS.

THE
City of Green Bay,
WISCONSIN.

AND ITS

History from its First Settlement up to the Present Time, including
Schools, Churches, Societies, Fire Department, &c..

It is not to be presumed that the few following pages, will contain the history of Green Bay, the oldest town in the State, one whose history runs back nearly one hundred and fifty years, demands a much larger space than the part of a Directory, and a worthier pen than ours when its history is to be written. We certainly have not the presumption to name ourselves as its historian. What we propose now to attempt, is a simple narration of the more prominent facts that have occurred in the gradual development of the city's growth, and to state as concisely as possible, the present condition as a basis of comparison for the future.

Going back, therefore, not to its first occupation by the white man, but to the first actual and permanent settlement by men that came to make it their home. We place as our first date the year 1745. When Augustine DeLanglade, with his son Charles, accompanied by a few others, some eighth in all, left Mackinaw and took up their abode on the present site of Green Bay. DeLanglade although

born of a noble family in France, had been impelled by his
love of adventure to come to America, and there marrying
the daughter of an Indian Chief, he had long lived among
the Indians, and was much respected by them. His son
Charles rose to great distinction as an Indian Officer during
the French and Indian war, that broke out soon after their
settlement at Green Bay. He will perhaps be best remem-
bered, from the fact of his having command of the Indian
forces in the celebrated defeat of Braddock. DeLanglade,
occupying about the same position in the French army, as
Washington did in the English. That is to say inferior in
command, but practically head. Throughout all that war
Chas. DeLanglade seemed to be present wherever there
was a battle. When peace was declared, he returned to his
home at Green Bay, for by the terms of the treaty, while
the forts and unoccupied land, passed into the possession of
the British Government, the settlers were allowed to hold
the claims that they had received from the French Government. The little coloney remained for many years in statu
quo. This was naturally the case from the character of the
colonists, they were not men of business enterprise, nor
were they eager to amass riches, they loved the wild life of
the woods, and the indolent freedom of the Indian. Charles
DeLanglade was a half-breed, and nearly all the settlers had
Indian wives. They were bold, courageous, and adventur-
ous, as befitted their peculiar positions, but used no boat
larger than a canoe, and raised no more grain than was
needed for their own consumption. For many years they
were content to grind their flour from a hand mill, turned
by two persons, then a horse-power increased their milling
facilities, so that they were able to grind fourteen bushels of
wheat in a day.

In 1785, forty years from its first settlement, the colony
could boast of but seven families, and fifty-six souls. Six-
teen out of these fifty-six, lived on the west side of the river,
the remainder of the population and the two stores, that
were then in operation were on the east side.

These early settlers living so far away from all civilized

life, and to all appearances, free from any nationality, were
nevertheless compelled from time to time, to be considered
the citizens of three different Nations. Originally owing al-
legiance to the French Government, they were transfered to
the power of the British, then at the close of the American
Revolution, they found themselves citizens of the United
States. This citizenship, however, they did not at that time
acknowledge, and in the war of 1812 considered themselves
upon the side of Great Brittan, and took arms against the
United States. At the close of that war, however, no re-
scourse was left them but to submit to the laws of the United
States. So slowly, however, had the settlement grown in
numbers, that up to 1812, nearly 80 years from its beginning,
there were not more than 250 souls living there. These
were almost all of French or Indian extraction.

    At a very early day the French had built a fort here, as a
protection against the Indians. This fort afterwards fell into
the hands of the English, together with the Post, and was
by them abandoned in 1763. After the war of 1812, Col.
Miller, with a detachment of United States troops on board
of three schooners, sailed into the Fox River to the astonish-
ment of the villagers, as never before had a vessel of that
size been seen on those waters. These troops immediately
set about the work of building a fort. This fort was erected
on the west side of the river, and named Fort Howard, afterwards giving its name to the city, which grew up about it.
Up to this time the general character of the settlement had
remained unchanged. The manners and customs of the inhabitants are thus described by Col. Childs, who came here
to live in 1820. *He says*: "There were quite a number of re-
spectable French families residing at the Bay when I arrived.
They were all engaged in the Indian trade under the American Fur Company, each cultivating a small quantity of land.
Their manners and customs were of the most primitive
character, they never used the yoke for their oxen; but, instead, fastened sicks across the oxen's horns to draw by, and
mostly used fortugs, rope made out of bark. Their plows
were very uncouth, the plow shares being about as large as a

smoothing iron, while the beam was about twelve feet long, with a pair of wheels near the fore end to keep it sufficiently elevated from the ground. They could not plow within fifteen feet of their fences. Their principal food was game, fish, and hulled corn. They caught large quantities of sturgeon and trout, and they made immense quantities of maple sugar. At the proper season in the Spring, the entire settlement would remove to their sugar camps; after remaining two months, each family making from eighth to ten hundred pounds."

From the building of the fort, may be dated the actual growth of the settlement. The advent of the first purely American settler, speedily wrought a change in the entire community. Thrift and energy took the place of the half-dead, half-civilized life that had heretofore characterized the village. Law and order were enforced, where before, the the rule of savage life alone prevailed. One of the first orders of the first judge was, that the inhabitants should be properly married, and nearly one-half of the inhabitants thereupon for the first time entered into a legal marriage contract, not however, without sore complaints against what they considered an unnecessary imposition.

The year 1825 marks an era in the history of the city, as during that year, the first newspaper published west of Lake Michigan, was issued from Green Bay under the name of *The Intelligencer*. A. G. Ellis and J. V. Suydam, being the editors. In this same year the first framed house, erected in Wisconsin, was built here for Judge Doty, the man who had compelled the inhabitants to get married. The village slowly increased in population, and in 1830, the present north ward of the city was laid out under the name of Navarino, and in 1835, the present south ward was laid out under the name of Astor, after the principal proprietor, John Jacob Astor, who was at the head of what was known as " The American Fur Company," a very powerful corporation that endeavored to monopolize all the Fur trade of the northwest. Navarino and Astor remained as rivals for the increasing trade of the settlement, until 1839, when the feeling of

rivalry was put aside, and the two villages became one corporation under the name of Green Bay. The total population of the combined settlements at this time, did not exceed
300 souls. From this time the population increased much
more rapidly. All the boats that came up the lake stopped
at Green Bay, bringing with them many permanent settlers.
And in 1854 the city charter was obtained from the legislature. But at this time, its increasing prosperity received a
check by the diversion of trade into new channels. The rapidly
rising cities of Milwaukee and Chicago absorbed nearly all
of the traffic, and for some years the tide of Green Bay's prosperity ran low. But with the opening of new routes of transportation, new life was infused into the business prospects of
the city. The first railroad that reached Green Bay, was the
Chicago and Northwestern, which having been pushed gradually north, arrived at Fort Howard in the fall of 1860. Up
to this date, the long winter had almost isolated the citizens
of the Bay from the rest of the world. The advent of this
first railroad was, on this account, hailed with great joy, and a
great impetus was given to trade. About this same time,
a company which had been formed under a grant from the
United States Government, commenced operations for the
purpose of improving the navigation of the Fox and Wisconsin rivers, endeavoring to open a water communication
between Green Bay and the Mississippi river. The great
importance of this work was apparent to all, who have ever
taken it into consideration.

The Fox and Wisconsin rivers afforded a natural channel,
the divide separating the two streams, was but a mile and a
half in width, and consisted of a sandy prairie, through which
a canal could be easily made. The main obstacle, was the
great length of the route which required improvement. The
company went boldy to work and pushed their improve-
ments to a completion, and in a few years, Green Bay was
put into direct communication with the Mississippi. Boats
drawing not more than three feet of water could run the
whole length of the route at all stages of water. This was
soon found to be insufficient to compete with the railroads,

4

and many efforts were made to increase the facilities for navigation.. At last the general Government was prevailed upon to assume the work. The old company was bought out in 1872, and the work of improvement was begun immediately, and in all probability will be continued, until a constant depth of five feet is obtained. The value of such a canal can hardly be estimated. The Lower Fox with its immense water-power, would soon rival the Merrimac in its manufacture of cotton fabrics, and far surpass it in the variety and number of other manufactories.

The following table of the power now available on this river, will give a good idea of its manufacturing capacities:

At Neenah and Menasha..........   3,000 horse-power
  "   Appleton.................... 11,500   "
  "   Cedars   3,000   "
  "   Little Chute.............. 11,500   "
  "   Kaukauna........ 14,500   "
  "   Rapid Croche...............   2,300   "
  "   Little Kaukauna.............   2,300   "
  "   Depere   2,300   "
                                   ————   "
      TOTAL..................... 50,400   "

This immense power is perfectly inexhaustable, and contained within a distance of 36 miles. Green Bay is the natural depot for the reception and distrubution of all the goods here manufactured. For Green Bay is not only a commercial center by means of its water ways, but the events of the last few years have also made it a railroad center. In 1872 the Chicago and Northwestern Railroad was extended from Fort Howard to Escanaba, forming the connecting link between Chicago and Lake Superior—a railroad from Escanaba to Marquette having been constructed some years previously. The opening of this road gave to Green Bay the whole of the northern mining and lumbering country for a market.

But what the citizens most keenly felt the necessity of, was a railroad to the west, which should connect them with the great grain producing States, and enable them to compete with Milwaukee and Chicago for the transportation of grain. In 1866 a charter was obtained for the Lake Pepin Railway Company, but it was not until 1871 that active work was put upon its construction. When the work was once fairly begun, however, it was rapidly pushed to a completion, and the road was opened to the Mississippi and in running order in 1873. Already the city has felt the great benefit of this new route, a benefit that will without doubt increase in direct ratio with its years.

In 1871, a railroad under the name of the Milwaukee and Northern Railway, began to push its way from Milwaukee in an air line towards the north. This road reached Green Bay in 1873, shortening the distance to Milwaukee 37 miles, and to Chicago 51 miles, besides opening a competing route to those points. Thus it will be seen, that Green Bay has now all that can be desired in the way of carrying facilities. Her iron arms of commerce radiate to all points of the compass. The broad lakes with their tributaries lie at her door. The 275 miles of natural and artificial channel that connect her with the Mississippi gives to her free access to that mighty stream and its vast system of tributaries.

What she now needs is men of means and enterprise, men with clear heads to plan, and bold hearts to execute. And the wealth of east and west would here meet in a common market, enriching the people, and building up the greatest commercial center of the north.

A few of the citizens have perceived these golden opportunities, and with what limited means they could command, have endeavored to divert hither some of the vast stream of trade that is constantly passing by to other less favorable localities. Their success will undoubtedly induce others to follow them, and when once the tide fairly sets in, Green Bay will rapidly rise to her proper station among the cities of the republic. The traditions of the old sleepy existence which she experienced for a hundred years have clung to her, and kept her back in the race, but each year finds her a little more free from their deadening influence, and more awake to her own best interests. When once she has freed herself from all these lazy habits, and is fully awake, then will come the vigorous bounds that will soon bring her even with her now more prosperous sisters.

It remains for us now to give in conclusion, a brief description of the city as it now is, situated upon a peninsular, formed by the Fox and East rivers, it presents the appearance of a compact and beautiful city. Its business streets are well paved with the Nicholson pavement, and many fine blocks of stores indicate the thrift and prosperity of the merchants. Its hotels are well kept, and are a source of comfort and satisfaction to many tourists and traveling men who visit the city. Socially, Green Bay has long ago made its reputation. It is renowned as one of the most hospitable cities of the north. This is the most valuable legacy left to her by the old ease loving, good natured, and hospitable settlers. The very dwellings tell of the comfort and true sociability that pervades the city, and wear an air of hospitality that invites one to enter and assures him of a hearty welcome. The numerous churches speak clearly of the morals of the city, and their full attendance on the Lord's day, gives a proof of the citizens, faith that cannot be denied. The schools are well conducted and an honor to the city. We defer speaking of them here, as a full description of them will be found elsewhere.

GREEN BAY & MISS. CANAL

for Steamboat Navigation, Locks 160×35 ft.

Estimated cost by Brev.Maj.Gen. G.K.Warren, Maj. U.S.E.
of improvement of Wis.River from his Survey of 1867

To secure reliable depth of 3 ft. $ 427,749.37
" 1 " $206,700.95
" 5 " 4,164,270.00

LAKE MICHIGAN

WISCONSIN

MINNESOTA

IOWA

MADISON

MILWAUKEE

FOND DU LAC

GREEN BAY

PORTAGE

LA CROSSE

ST. JOHN'S CATHOLIC CHURCH.

The early history of the Roman Catholic Church in the city of Green Bay, and that of the city proper, are so closely blended as to almost entirely forbid any elimination in treating of either the one or the other. In truth that of the church, is the history of the northwest in early ages, and presents a field of investigation rich in resources, and we who now see it as it is, can scarcely in imagination carry ourselves back to those primeval times, when the only human voice that broke the stillness of the forest, was the war-whoop of the Indian. And as we read the written history of the early pioneers of the Catholic faith in this territory, we pause in silent admiration of the zeal which prompted them to brave the hardships and dangers of those times. Supported by no human sympathy for their toil and suffering, with no eye to pity, no arm to save, they looked not to human praise for their reward. Filled with zeal for their cause, with love for their fellow man, and trusting entirely upon the all sustaining arm of Him whom they served, they literally gave their dust to dust, and ashes to ashes.

The earliest advent of the Jesuit Missionaries, into the country west of Detroit, seems to have been that of Nicolet, in the year 1640, who then visited what was known as the " Sea Tribe," supposed to be the Winnebagoes of Green Bay, and with whom he seems to have concluded a treaty in the name of France. Other missions were quickly established in diffrent parts of the territory, but it was not until the year 1669, that any permanent mission was organized in Green Bay. In December of that year, Father Alloues having left Father Marquette in charge of the mission at Lapoint, came to Green Bay, and celebrating his first mass on the festival of St. Francies Xavier called the mission by his name. In 1671, owing to the war which broke out

5

between the Sioux on the one hand, and the Ottawas and
Hurons on the other, the Dacotas sent back to Marquette his
books and pictures and declared war. Further progress by
Lake Superior being now closed by this war, Green Bay became the chief hope of the missionaries, since through it, by
the Fox River, they hoped to reach new nations. In 1672,
the mission house during the absence of its missionary Andre,
was destroyed by fire, but soon rebuilt upon the ruins of the
old, and in the year 1678, we find him directing his little
church of 500 christians, which slowly but gradually increased. A fine church had been erected by the Rapide des-
Peres, partly it would seem by the aid of wester traders,
among whom was Nicholas Perrot, one of the early western
explorers. The present parish has now in its possession a
silver remonstrance, which bears the following inscription
upon the base, evidently made with a knife.

" This remonstrance was presented by Mr. Nicholas Perrot, to the Mission of St. Francis Xavier, in the *Bay de
puants* 1686."

In 1680 Father Enjalran was in charge of the mission in
Green Bay, which he seemed to have retained until 1688.
From here all trace is lost, and nothing is placed upon record
to tell its fate. In 1700, we find that Father Enjalran then
at Quebec, was sent to induce the western tribes to appear at
the great congress of 1701.

At that epoch we learn, that several missionaries were still
on the Ottawa mission, among whom were Father J. Marest,
but of their respective stations we have no tidings, and in
1706, missionaries at Mackinaw, finding it useless to continue
their efforts, burned their house and chapel, and returned to
Quebec. Soon after, Father J. J. Marest was induced to return, and in 1711, we find him superior of the Ottawa and
Illinois missions.

In 1721, but two missionaries seem to have been engaged in
the Ottawa mission, one at the Sault, and the other Father
Chardon at Green Bay. Subsequently, the Indian wars
plunged the west into disorder, and little is known of the
Ottawa mission, until the time of the last Jesuite missionaries

among the western tribes, and the whole mission devolved upon Marin Louis Lefrance, and Peter Janny, who were stationed at Mackinaw until 1765. Thus closed for the time, the labors of these truly great and good men—men who had endured almost any hardship, feeling themselves well repaid for their labor, if they succeeded in the baptism of a single savage. Nor was their work useless; as late as the year 1820, aged men among the Indians were wont to breathe benedictions upon their heads, and point out the spot where they were accustomed to say their breviary.

After the close of the American revolution, attention was again called to these Indian missions, and in 1821, Gabriel Richard then stationed at Detroit, visited the missions upon the shore of Michigan, and also visited the posts of Drummond Island, Mackinaw, Sault St. Mary's and Green Bay.

In 1827, Dejean arrived in Mackinaw, and he soon had the satisfaction of seeing his efforts crowned with success. In 1830 Rev. Frederic Reze, reached Green Bay, and baptized a number of the Menomonees who had been previously instructed, and soon under the management of Mazzuchelli & Vendenbroeck, became the mother parish to many in the vicinity. Thus was permanently established what now forms the Parish of St. John. A small woden shanty was procured, and in it for sometime were held the services of the church. This stood on grounds in what is now termed "shanty-town", and being destroyed by fire, a building which then stood on the lot adjoining that on which the church now stands, was purchased of the Methodist Society, and having been enlarged, became the home of the parish.

From that time its growth has been rapid and permanent, and about the year 1848, the German portion of the parish, organized their present church of St. Mary's, and is now in a flourishing condition, it being the home of the Bishop, as also the cathedral. About the year 1860, the Irish portion of the church organized their society, and established themselves as such in Fort Howard; and about three years later, the Holland and Flemish portion erected their present church edifice, and now worship there, leaving the present St.

John's, as a French Catholic Church. In 1871 the old
house, belonging to the society, was destroyed by fire. The
erection of the present structure was commenced immediately
thereafter, and completed in 1872. It is a handsome brick
structure 132 feet in length, by 58 in width, on either corner
of the south end are located square towers rising high in the air,
rendering the church a conspicuous one from any portion of
the city. It has a seating capacity, including gallery, nearly
1500, and was erected at a cost of about $20,000. The parish
now has a membership of 340 families, giving a congregation
of about 1300, and is under the pastoral care of its very efficient Pastor, P. Crude, is in a flourishing condition.

ST. MARY'S CHURCH.

As has before been stated, this church was organized about
twenty-five years since, by the German portion of St. John's
Church, since which time they have been an independent
organization. Commencing with but a few members, its
growth has been rapid, and in 1868 the Bishop made it a
cathedral, and here has his home. In connection herewith is
also the St. Mary's Parochial School. The Bishop's house is
a very neat and appropriate building, located on corner of
Madison and Doty streets. The see, vacated by the death of
the late Bishop, in September 1873, is yet unsupplied, and
hence, the duties pertaining to that office, so far as they may
be, are performed by the Rev. E. Daems as administrator of
the Diocese. The cathedral proper, is under the pastoral
care of Rev. A. N. Bushnell, with Rev. J. O'Brien assistant,
and although having recently become the mother parish of
the Polish Catholic Church, now numbers about 1500. The
limited capacity of the cathedral building has necessitated a
division of the congregation, and services are held a follows:
Private mass at 8 A. M., at 9 A. M. with sermon, High
Mass with sermon at 10 A. M., and vespers at 2:30 P. M.

ST. WILLEBRORD'S HOLLAND CATHOLIC CHURCH.

Located on southeast corner of Adams and Doty streets. Parsonage one door south of church.

Services—First Mass 8 A. M. in Winter, and 7 A. M. in Summer, High Mass 10 A. M. in Winter, and 9 A. M. in Summer, Vespers 3 P. M., Sunday School 2. P. M.

The congregation of this church formerly belonged to to that of St. Mary's German Church, but in 1864, the congregation had become so large as to require either its division, or the erection of a larger building. It was decided by the Holland portion of the church to separate from St. Mary's, which they did in the same year with the approbation of Bishop Henni of Milwaukee. They purchased the old Court House of Green Bay for $300, and the lot the church now occupies for $1200. In 1865 an addition was made to the church building, costing $900, but it not yet being of sufficient capacity, another addition was made, and vestry-room built, costing $1200, in 1869, so that at the present time the edifice is large enough to accommodate those who worship there. In the same year that the last addition was made to the church, a parsonage was built of brick, costing $3,200, and the lot which it occupies purchased at $1,500.

The church is built of wood, und is 95 feet in length, by 30 in width, with a capacity for seating 400.

When this congregation separated from St. Mary's Church, it numbered 45 families; now it has increased to nearly 120.

St. Willebrord's is under the pastoral care of the Rev. Father Hoffen.

CHRIST CHURCH. (P. EPISCOPAL)

Located on northwest corner of Cherry and Madison sts. Rev. M. V. Averill, Rector. Rectory, No. 101 Cherry. Services Sunday at 10:30 A. M., and 7:30 P. M.

In 1823 the Rev. Eleazer Williams, then a missionary, visited Green Bay and performed the first services of the Church, in a log school house, which then stood on or near the grounds, now known as the farm of L. Grignon. In September of 1829, was organized the Parish of Christ Church, which was duly incorporated by the Legislature of Michigan, in October following, with the Rev. R. F. Cadle as Rector, Daniel Whitney and Albert G. Ellis, Wardens; Jas. D. Doty, William Dickensen. John Lawe, A. J. Irwin, J. P. Arndt, S. W. Beale, R. Irwin, Jr., and H. S. Baird as Vestry-men. This was the first Parish organized in the Diocese, and to her must we accord the proud dis- tinction " The Mother Parish."

In 1830, the Rev. R. F. Cadle, acquired the title to a piece of land lying on the Fox River, between Green Bay and Depere, in the name of the Domestic and Foreign Missionary Society, and erected, as agent of that society, buildings, and established a school and mission. This then became the home of the infant parish, and so remained until 1832, when a school building having been fitted up for the purpose, in what was then the town of Navarino, was used as a church. This building is still standing, and forms a portion of a busi- ness block, located on south side of Cherry, between Wash- ington and Adams street.

In 1848 was erected the present church edifice, and is now among the oldest in the city.

In 1866, the ladies of the parish organized a society, which was called the " Society of the Woman of Christ Church, and had for its object the establishment of a home for friend- less and destitute persons, an account of which will be seen under the head of Cadle Home; and in 1872 was organized, by a portion of the members of this parish, the present parish of St. James.

The church now under the fostering care of the Rev. M. V. Averill, is in a flourishing condition, has about 106 communicants, a congregation of 375, and property valued at $20,000.

ST. JAMES CHURCH (EPISCOPAL.)

As has been previously stated, this parish was organized in 1872, by a portion of the parish of Christ Church. Services were held in Whites Hall until a few weeks ago, since which time they have been held in the first ward school house.

They have now in process of erection, a beautiful church edifice, at a cost of about $15,000, which, when completed, will be an ornament to the city, as well as a credit to the society. It is located on Monroe street near the south limits of the city, on an elevated plateau of ground, overlooking the greater part of the city; a more beautiful location could scarcely have been selected.

The parish is in a very flourishing condition, with communicants numbering about 40, and a congregation of about 100. It is under the Rectorship of Rev. R. F. Haff, whose residence is west side of Quincy, second north of Crooks. Services Sunday at 10:30 A. M.

THE FIRST PRESBYTERIAN CHURCH IN GREEN BAY.

Pastor, Rev. William Crawford. Residence corner of Adams and Crooks street. Hours of service, 10:30 A. M., and 7:30 P. M., Sabbath School 12 M., Prayer meeting, Wednesday 7:30 P. M. Young people's meeting, Monday 7:30 P. M.

This church was organized January 9th, 1836, with twelve members. Its present membership is 164. Its property consists of one-fourth of a block, with house of worship and parsonage, at the corner of Adams and Crooks streets. The house of worship will seat about 350, and measures have been taken to enlarge it by 120 sittings.

During the past year 296 have been enrolled in the Sabbath School. Superintendent, Mr. L. W. Briggs. The S.

S. Library contains 525 volumes, and is under the charge of Messrs. J. M. Norris and C. W. Vroman. A branch school under the superintendence of Mr. W. S. Butler, is held at Oak Grove at 3 P. M.

For the year ending August 1st, 1874, the amount raised for the support of the Gospel in Green Bay, was $2,847.43, and for charities, $422.33.

FRENCH PRESBYTERIAN CHURCH.

Located on north side of Doty, between Adams and Jefferson streets.

Services every Sunday, 10:30 and 7:30.

Rev. L. Levasseur, Pastor. As has before been stated, this society recently purchased their present church building of the German Methodist Society, and although yet an infant organization having but about 40 members, it presents a vigorous growth.

CENTRAL, (BAPTIST) CHURCH.

The Central Baptist Church of Green Bay, is located on the southwest corner of Madison and Moravian streets; was organized in 1867 with ten members; it was without a permanent place of worship until September 1873, when its present chapel was dedicated. In November 1873, Rev. J G. Henshall, M. D. was called to pastorate, and is still laboring in that capacity, his residence is 526 Main street.

The present membership is thirty-three. Cost of Chapel $3,500.

𝕽eal 𝕰state Office

OF

A. GUESNIER,

ESTABLISHED 1862.

𝕷ands & 𝕮ity 𝕷ots

BOUGHT AND SOLD.

LOANS NEGOTIATED,

MONEY INVESTED.

TAXES PAID &C.

GREEN BAY, WISCONSIN.t

Hours of worship on Sunday, 10:30 A. M., 7:30 P. M., Sunday School at 12 M.

Communion on the first Sunday in every month. Prayer and Conference meeting every Wednesday evening, at 7½ o'clock.

METHODIST CHURCH.

Madison Street Methodist Episcopal Church, located on the corner of Madison and School streets. Rev. James M. Walker, Pastor, residence 200 Madison street.

Services Sunday 10:30 A. M., and 7:30 P. M.

The first services of this church, were held in the city of Green Bay about the year 1832, by the Rev. J. M. Clark, who was sent here as a missionary from New York. Its prosperity has never been very marked, and although they have property valued at about $10,000, and are financially well situated, they have a membership of only about 27. This number, however, under the pastoral care of the present minister, will no doubt be greatly increased in the near future.

GERMAN METHODIST SOCIETY.

This society was first organized as a mission in 1860, when subsequently a small house of worship was erected on north side of Doty, between Adams and Jefferson streets. This has recently been sold to the French Presbyterian Congregation, and the society have in contemplation the erection of a church building, on the corner of Doty and Clay street, contiguous to their parsonage.

7

This society is now in a flourishing condition, with about 60 members, under the care of the Rev. Wm. Hoekle. Services every Sunday at 10:30 A. M. and 7:30 P. M.

- • -

ST. MARY'S PAROCHIAL SCHOOL.

Corner of Monroe and Doty streets.

This school was organized in December 1872, by the Rev. Father F. X. Pfaller, then in charge of St. Mary's Church, by procuring the aid of teachers from the Mother Superior at Milwaukee. Its object is that of teaching the children of both sexes of all religious belief, the common branches of education, although a restriction is made against boys over 12 years of age. Needle work is also taught twice during the week, while the price of tuition is merely nominal. Commencing with only 35 scholars, it has now over 300 in attendance, and is under the immediate management of Sisters of Notre Dame, and relatively that of St. Mary's Parish, the efficiency of which can be seen by increase of attendance.

- • -

URSALINE ACADEMY.

A school for girls, south east corner of Webster and Crooks street. This is in all respects similar to that of St. Mary's Parochial School, except it is for girls only, and under the management of Sisters of Order of St. Ursaline. It has an attendance of about 30 scholars, which number is constantly increasing.

PUBLIC SCHOOLS.

The schools of the City are under the management and direction of a Board of Seven Commissioners, elected by the City Council. The board yearly elect one of their number President, and such other person Superintendent as they may deem qualified, who acts as Secretary.

In each of the three wards of the city is a school, accomodating the Primary and Intermediate Departments. Centrally located is the High School, with the Grammar Department. With but one exception, (Principal of High School,) all the departments are in charge of female teachers.

The school buildings will compare favorably with any in the State, being well built, conveniently arranged, seated with single desks and kept in good condition.

The Board of Education holds monthly meetings, at which usually every member is present, giving careful attention to all matters brought up, pertaining to the interests of the schools.

A clearly defined course of study has been adopted, and the Primary and Intermediate Departments are thoroughly graded.

In the High School, a comprehensive course of study is followed as closely as is practicable.

L. W. Briggs, *Principal High School*; Miss Ida Gordon, *Assistant.*

GRAMMAR DEPARTMENT.

Miss L. V. Alban, *Principal*; Miss Julia White *Assistant.*

1ST WARD, INTERMEDIATE AND PRIMARY DEPARTMENT.

Miss C. A. Burritt, *Principal*; Miss Adelade Sutton, 3d *Primary Department*; Miss Emma R. Briggs, 2d *Primary Department*; Miss Sarah E. Paderson, 1st *Primary Department.*

PINE STREET, INTERMEDIATE AND PRIMARY DEPARTMENT.

Miss M. J. Rider, *Principal*; Miss Fannie M. Thornton, 3d *Department*; Miss Millie Wight, 2d *Department*; Miss Zada March, 2d *Department*; Miss Sarah D. Hamilton, 2d *Department*; Miss M. L. Burns, 1st *Department.*

Miss Mary E. Ferris, *Principal*; Miss Bell M. Smith , *Assistant.*

E. H. ELLSWORTH, *Superintendent.*

CADLE HOME.

In the year 1866, the ladies of Christ Church, formed a society, for the purpose of procuring a home for orphans and for the friendless and the destitute. With so noble an object in view, it could not prove other than successful. It is true difficulties had to be overcome, and trials endured but they had their recompense in the relief afforded the suffering and destitute. Beginning with no available means, and relying wholly upon the benevolence of its members, and the charitable offerings of others, its first year showed an income of nearly one thousand dollars, which was immediately disbursed in the needs of the society. '

In this manner it continued until the year 1870, when the late Bishop Armitage, succeeded in procuring a deed from the " Domestic and Foreign Missionary Society," of what is now known as the mission farm, in favor of the " Trustees of Funds and Property of the Diocese of Wisconsin," to be held by them for the benefit of the Church Home in Green Bay. In addition to this, in the following year, the surplus of money remaining in the hands of Bishop Armitage, and the Rev. R. W. Blow, then rector of Christ Church, and which had been donated in aid of the sufferers, by the fire in Northern Wisconsin, was with the consent of the donors, transferred to the society, and was the first pecuniary aid they received in of establishing the Home. In 1872 the " Cadle Home" was duly organized in accordance with the General Laws of the State.

Its objects were briefly stated to be, " for the purpose of

erecting, establishing and maintaining a home and hospital for the education and maintenance of orphan children, for the care and relief of sick, infirm, needy, destitute or homeless persons, for the care and support of aged and infirm clergymen, or for any or all of these, or such other charitable purposes as this corponation may from time to time undertake to carry into execution."

In January 1874, the society completed their present building upon the grounds procured for that purpose. Eventually this will be used for an asylum, while buildings for hospital purposes will be erected on the mission farm.

The Home is not a local organization, nor are its benefits to be confined to the Protestant Episcopal Church, while it will be under its management, it intends to furnish relief to the homeless and destitute irrespective of any creed.

PHILHARMONIC SOCIETY.

We regret that the limits of our work, prevent us giving a lengthy account of this society.

Organized with the laudable purpose of cultivating the most beautiful of all arts, music, its success can be foretold with almost unerring certainty. In truth it is an art which brings its own reward, for who that has feeling, ever listened to its ravishing strains unmoved? and when aided by that energetic perseverence, and laudable desire to excel, so characteristic of the members of this society, its perfect rendition is only a question of time. We have not had the pleasure of listening to the society's rendition of any of its Oratorias or Cantatas, but judging from what we have seen and heard at its recent rehearsals, are convinced that it has a fore most place among the similar societies of the northwest. Its examples should be followed by the organization of societies in many other cities, and thus call into more active being, the sweet concord

8

of soul and purpose, making life purer and better by its ennobling and soothing influence. Let us hope its harmony may always be as perfect as that of its music, and no discordant sounds, ever break its sweetly swelling strains. Great credit is due Mr. G. L. North, its efficient conductor for the high standard the society has attained, and to those who have so nobly sustained him in his efforts in its behalf. We should be glad to particularize in favor of many of its members, but space forbids, and herewith give the report of the society, which conveys in language, far stronger than ours, the estimation in which it is held.

PHILHARMONIC ANNIVERSARY.—" August the third" is a notable day in history. It was on that memorable day that " *Ah Sin*" the " heathen Chinee" achieved his wonderful success at Euchre, " the game he did *not* understand." It was also on " August the third" 1872, that the Philharmonic Society of this city had its birth, and the success achieved by the society in the past two years, is quite as remarkable as the wonderful advancement of *Ah Sin*.

The society on last Monday entered upon its third year, and a condensed statement of its condition, taken from the more detailed accounts, rendered by the Secretary and Treasurer, may not be uninteresting.

The Treasurer reports that the society has received since the organization in August 1872, the sum of $1,594.59. As this has nearly all come from our own people, and those living in neighboring places, we append a list of the sources from which it came:

From the Esther Concerts, four nights, $716.73
From the First Miscellaneous concert, $225.75.
From the First Belshazzar concert, four nights, $834.90
From the Concert by Bach's Orchestra, $237.18.
From the Second Miscellaneous concert, $200.75.
From the Third Miscellaneous concert, $203.05.
From the Second Belshazzar concert, four nights, $1,003.65.

From Honorary Members two years, $730.

The balance of the amount as given above has been received from the initiations and dues of Active Members.

The Secretary reports that there are now on the rolls of the society, the names of one-hundred and twenty-five *live* Active Members. This does not include those who have withdrawn from the society.

The statement of the Treasurer showed, that although the expenses of the society have been enormous, there remains on hand and due from active members, nearly one-hundred dollars; and that all accounts against the society, from whatever source, have been paid. This, considering the fact that the society is the possessor of a fine eight-hundred-dollar Chickering piano, and music and books which cost them about two-hundred dollars, is a very flattering exhibit.

It was decided to resume the weekly rehearsals, which will be held in Turners' Hall, every Tuesday evening.

The following persons were elected as a Board of Management for the ensuing year:

OFFICERS.

President,................A. W. KIMBALL.
Vice-President,...........GEO. W. WATSON
Secretary,..................W. C. BAILEY.
Treasurer,...................J. F. GOODING.
Conductor,................GEO. L. NORTH. ·
Librarian,..................C. T. KIMBALL.

DIRECTORS.

OLIVER LIBBEY,.........M. V. B. BENSON.
JNO. D. WILLIAMS.........H. G. FREEMAN.
L. W. BRIGGS,... ....M. H. WALKER.

GREEN BAY LODGE, NO. 19, I. O. O. F.

This Lodge was instituted July 14th, 1847, by Special Deputy, Herman L. Page, then Grand Marshal, under a Dis-

pensation issued by Grand Master John D. Kinsman. It is
an interesting incident of its history that Hope No. 17,
Friendship No. 18, and Green Bay No. 19, were the first
three Lodges instituted by authority of the Grand Lodge of
Wisconsin, and these three were authorized by one, and the
same resolution, adopted on the 10th day of June, 1847, the
very next day after the institution of the Grand Lodge itself.
Thus was Green Bay Lodge coupled, in the very hour of
her conception, with her lovely twin sisters, Hope and Friendship, and the triplet became the first born daughters of our
now prominent and powerful Grand Jurisdiction.

Its charter members were Timothy O. Howe, Henry
O.Scholtz, Henry S. Baird, Daniel W. King, John Day, and
Charles L. Wheelock, the last one of whom still retains his
active membership in the Lodge. The institution took place
in the building now known as the Bay City House, on the
corner of Walnut and Washington streets. The first officers
installed were H. S. Baird, N. G.; H. O. Scholtz, V. G.; J.
V. Suydam, *Secretary*; G. S. Armstrong, *Treasurer*; T. C.
Morgan, W.; T. O. Howe, C.; E. S. Disbrow, R. S. N. G.;
D. W. King, L. S. N. G.; C. L. Wheelock, R. S. V. G.;
John Day, L. S. V. G.: E. Hart, I. G.; T. Bennett, O. G.;
A. C. Robinson, R. S. S.; J. W. Arndt, L. S. S.

On the evening of institution, and previously thereto, nine
applicants were initiated into the Order under Dispensation,
among whom were H. S. Baird, H. O. Scholtz, D. W. King
and C. L. Wheelock.

Of the first 16 years of its existence, nothing is on record
pertaining to Green Bay Lodge, save the statistical items, and
other occasional references to it in the proceedings of the
Grand Lodge. During this interval the Lodge suffered some
serious misfortunes. Once it was burned out; and at another
time it lost all the funds in its treasury $800 by theft.

On the 11th of November 1863, every vestige of the
the Lodge, except its living members, was again swept away
by the destructive conflagration that annihilated so much of
the business portion of the city.

This last and greatest disaster, instead of disheartening the

Brothers, served rather to rouse their energies, and give new impetus to their associated endeavors. Not a single session of the Lodge was omitted, but on the 17th, six days after the fire, the regular meeting was held in the Masonic Hall, generously tendered them, " for such a period as their necessities might require." Go on was the prompt, unhesitating and unanimous voice of the Lodge—and it has gone on, from that day to this, multiplying in numbers, increasing in power and influence, and doing its appropriate works of beneficence, till now it ranks among the first Lodges of the Jurisdiction, numbering 130 active members, and possessing in common with Hermann Lodge No 111, the handsomely furnished hall, corner of Adams and Cherry streets, together with cash funds and other property, entirely its own, to the value of about $2,500.

Green Bay Lodge, besides contributing " more than its share of members," on the institution of the Lodges at Fond-du Lac, Oshkosh and Waupun, has regularly " swarmed" three times, the " hived" results being Hermann No. 111, Oconto No. 190, and DePere No. 222.

This Lodge has the honor of having supplied to the Grand Lodge one Grand Master and Grand Representative, the Hon. M. P. Lindsley, and to the Grand Encampment one Grand Patriarch, Prof. Werden Reynolds, the latter gentleman being also the compiler of the Wisconsin Digest.

The Lodge holds its regular meetings on Tuesday of each week.

HERMANN LODGE, I. O. O. F.

Hermann Lodge No. 111. I. O. O. F., was instituted March 7th, 1866, by D. D. Grand Master B. C. Gardner. Charter members Louis Scheller, Robert Graner, Joseph Nick, F. Charles Jansen, Ernest Straubel, August Strauhel.

9

First elective officers, Louis Scheller, N. G.; Robert Graner, V. G.; F. Charles Jansen, *Secretary*; Earnest Straubel *Treasurer.* The Lodge has enjoyed an uninterrupted course of harmony and prosperity from the first, and embraces among its members, some of the worthiest and most intelligent of our German citizens. It numbers about 80 members, owns equal interest with Green Bay Lodge in Odd Fellows Hall on Cherry street, and has in cash funds at the present date, about $2,400, with $225 worth of regalia and fixtures.

The present officers are Charles Hartung, N. G.; Hillmar Danz, V. G.; F. Charles Jansen, *Secretary*, Edward Kittner, *Treasurer.*

Its regular meetings are held on Wednesday evening of each week.

SARAH LODGE, No. 16, I. O. O. F.

Of the Rebekah Degree was chartered January 19th, 1871, with nine Brothers and ten Sisters. It works in the German Language, and holds monthly meetings on the second Friday of each month, in Odd Fellows Hall.

GOLDEN RULE ENCAMPMENT, No. 18, I. O. O. F.

Was instituted April 25th, 1867, by M. W. Grand Patriarch D. S, Morse, assisted by Grand Scribe, L. B. Hills, D. D., Grand Patriarch Sam Ryan, Jr., and other distinguished Brethern of the Order.

Its Charter members were M. P. Lindsley, H. Martin, J. A. Pinto, O. B. Graves, C. C. Lovett, B. C. Gardner, Werden

Reynolds, E. C. Keeler, and T. J. Bailey. The first elective officers installed were J. A. Pinto, C. P.; M. P. Lindsley, H. P.; B. C. Gardner, S. W.; Werden Reynolds, *Scribe*; H. Martin *Treasurer*; C. C. Lovett, J. W.

Five applicants from Green Bay Lodge were admitted, and all the Degrees were conferred upon them immediately upon the organization of the Encampment. Its present membership is about 50.

It holds semi-monthly meetings on the first and third Fridays of each month, in Odd Fellows Hall.

WASHINGTON LODGE, No. 21, F. & A. M.

Nights of meetings, 1st and 3d Thursdays of every month.

OFFICERS.

A. W. Kimball, W. M.; M. F. Greeley, S. W.; W. E. Thomas, J. W.; D. W. King, *Treasurer*; J. M. Norris, *Secretary*.

WARREN CHAPTER, No. 8.

Meets 2d and 4th Mondays of every month.

OFFICERS.

C. E. Crane, H. P.; Oliver Libbey, K.; J. H. Elmore, S.

BOHEMIAN AID AND EDUCATIONAL SOCIETY.

This society was organized June 16th, 1862, and as its name indicates, is a benevolent one. Its object being mutual improvement in the common branches of the English and Bo-

hemian Languages, and the relief of sick and indigent members. It is not a secret society, and is open to all Bohemians
who may choose to enter. In case of sickness a weekly
compensation of four dollars is paid out of the society fund,
and in case more is needed, it is paid by contribution, its
Treasury being supplied by annual dues. They now have a
mebership of 23.

Its officers are John Safranek, *President*; Anton Cech, *Secretary*; W. Peck, *Treasurer*.

POST OFFICE.

The Post Office is located on the west side of Adams, between Pine and Cherry streets, convenient to the business
portion of the city. Few if any, that we have seen, are so
completely arranged for the accommodation of the public, and
the rapid transaction of its increasing business as this.
Nearly thirteen hundred boxes and drawers are arranged for
the convenience of its patrons, and the extent of its business
may be approximated, when we consider the fact that nearly
65,000 letters are transmitted through it during each month,
in addition to several tons of printed matter.

The Money Order Department showed receipts and pay-
ments for the month of June, of $9,026.89, and is constantly
on the increase.

Too much praise cannot be accorded to Mr. W. C. E.
Thomas the present P. M., for his able management, and the
thanks of the community are due Messrs. W. E. Thomas,
Chas. H. Briot, and the remainder of the force, for their
gentlemanly and courteous attention.

Office Hours, General Delivery 8 A. M. to 7:30 P. M.
Lock Boxes 6 A. M. to 11 P. M. Sunday 9 A. M. to 10
A. M. Money Order Office excepting Sunday, 8 A. M. to
6 P. M.

CITY GOVERNMENT.

OFFICERS AND COMMITTEES.

Charles E. Crane, *Mayor*; J. D. Williams, *President of Council*; C. Vroman, *Attorney*; Frank Lenz, *Treasurer*; Jule R. Morris, *Clerk*.

MEMBERS OF COMMON COUNCIL.

First Ward—W. Parish, J. D. Williams, Mathias Miller.
Second Ward—A. G. E. Holmes, Albert Weise, C. Meister.
Third Ward—C. W. Hendricks, C. Woelz, A. Seibel.

SUPERVISORS.

First Ward—J. B. Jacobs; Second Ward—Fred S. Ellis; Third Ward—J. V. Suydam.

POLICEMEN.

J. A. Killian, *Chief*; G. Bong, G. Biemeret, F. Piero, A. Gehrke and T. Mahn.

FIRE WARDENS.

John B. Jacobs and J. F. Loy, First Ward; F. S. Ellis and A. W· Kimball, Second Ward; Henry Rahr and J. Whitney, Third Ward.

BOARD OF HEALTH.

William Scott and W. R. Bourne, First Ward; P. Marchand and J. S. Featherly, Second Ward; C. Berner and M. Resch, Third Ward.

COMMITTEES.

Finance—J. D. Williams, A. Weise and C. Woelz.
Accounts—C. Woelz, A. G. E. Holmes and W. Parish.
Ordinances—A. Seibel, C. Meister and W. Parish.
Fire Department—C. Meister, A. Seibel and J. D. Williams.
Printing—A. Seibel, C. Meister and M. Miller.
Streets and Bridges—A. Weise, C. Woelz and M. Miller.
Taverns and Groceries—A. G. E. Holmes, C. W. Hendricks and W. Parish.
Public Grounds—C. W. Hendricks, C. Meister and M. Miller.
Gas Lights—W. Parish, A. G. E. Holmes and C. Meister.
Chief Engineer of Fire Department—Louis Scheller.

1D

COUNTY OFFICERS.

E. Holmes Ellis, *Circuit Judge*; David Agry, *Probate Judge*; John J. Tracy, *District Attorney*; John B. A. Massie, *Clerk of Court*; E. Crocker, *Sheriff*; Frank Van Stralen, *Treasurer*; Geo. W. Watson, *Register*; M. J. Mead, *Clerk of Board*; S. E. Baldwin, *County Surveyor*.

FIRE DEPARTMENT.

L. Scheller, *Chief Engineer*; C. D. Suydam, *Assistant Chief Engineer*.

Few cities, if any, of like size can boast of a better Fire Department than Green Bay. During our stay we had the privilege of seeing its practical working, and are free to say, that it seems to be ably and efficiently managed. The water supply for the principal business thoroughfare is the Fox River, while the residence portion is provided with seven reservoirs, fed by springs, giving in most sections, an ample supply for at least ordinary fires. The Fire Department consists of two steamers and two hand engines, and are manned by four companies.

ASTOR NO. I, (HAND ENGINE,)

Has about 35 members, with John Jacob, Jr., *Foreman*; Anton Masse, *Secretary*.

GERMANIA NO. 2, (STEAMER ENTERPRISE.)

The engine is an " Amoskeag," of second class and in fine working order. It is manned by about 25 members, with Aug. Brauns as *Foreman*; G. Bong as *Secretary*. J. F. Berttes the Engineer, is eminently qualified for his position, and has in addition to his immediate duties as engineer of the Enterprise, the superintendency of the mechanical portion of the department. The perfect working of the apparatus, speak in strong language of his ability for this important trust.

GUARDIAN NO. 2, (STEAMER GUARDIAN.)

This is a " Clapp & Jones" engine of third class, and is also manned by a company of 25 members. With L. Dennis as Engineer is always on hand, always ready to perform its full share of the duties, and is under Foremanship of C. W. Tracy, while Secretaryship is held by F. W. Basche.

FRANKLIN CO., NO. 3, (HAND ENGINE.)

This company numbers 35 members, although compelled to draw their engine cy hand, are generally among the first to reach the scene of action. They are a fine body of men, and in excellent drill. John Nic, *Foreman*.

WARD BOUNDARIES.

The First Ward comprises all that portion of the city of Green Bay, bounded on the south by city limits, west by Fox River, north by a line drawn equidistant between Chicago and Crooks streets, and east by East River.

Second Ward constitutes that portion, bounded on the south by line equidistant between Chicago and Crooks sts., west by Fox River, north by a line midway between Pine and Cherry streets, to intersection of Eleventh, thence north and east to East River, east by Newburry Tract and East River.

Third Ward, bounded south by above described north line of Second Ward, west by Fox River, north by city limits, being south line of Harvey street, and east by Pleasant street.

STREET DIRECTORY.

Fox River on the west of the city, is taken as a guide for streets running north and south, and all streets are numbered from it as they intersect Main and Crooks streets. Walnut street being that upon which is located the north bridge of the Fox River, is taken as a guide for the streets intersecting it, and are numbered north and south from it.

Adams street, 2d east of Fox River, extends from River north, to Polier south.

Baird street, 13th north of Fox River, extends from north to south limits.

Cass street, 6th south of Walnut, and 6th north of south limits, extends from Fox River west to East River east.

Cedar street, 4th north of Walnut, extends from Fox Rive west to Quincy east, thence follows bend of river to Clayr thence across River to east limits.

Cherry street, 1st north of Walnut, extends from Fox River on the west, to city limits east.

Chicago street, 4th south of Walnut extends from Fox River to city limits, and is intercepted between Jefferson and Madison by Calhoun square.

Clay street, 10th east of Fox River.

Congress street, short street, south side of Webster square

Crooks street, 3d south of Walnut, extends from Fox River to city limits, between Madison and Monroe.

Doty street, 1st south of Walnut, from Fox River to city limits east.

Eleventh street, 11th east of Fox River.

Eliza street, 9th south of Walnut, 3d north of south city limits.

Elm street, 5th north of Walnut, or 2d north of Main, from Adams to Monroe.

Emilie street, 10th south of Walnut, 2d north of south city limits, extende from Fox River to East River.

Goodell street, 14th north of Fox River, on Crooks, extends from Crooks to city limits.

Grignon street, 11th south of Walnut, 1st north of south limits, extends from Fox River to East River.

Howard street, short street, south side Calhoun square.

Jackson street, 7th east of Fox River.

Jefferson street, 3d east of Fox River.

Lawe street, 7th south of Walnut, 5th north of south limits, intercepted by Webster square.

Madison street, 4th east of Fox River.

Main street, 3d north of Walnut, from Fox River to city limits

Mason street, 5th south of Walnut, extends from Fox River to East River.

Milwaukee street, short street, south side of Calhoun square.

Monroe street, 5th north of Fox River.

Moravian street, short street, south side of Jackson square.

Pine street, 2d north of Walnut, extends from Fox to East River.

Polier street, 8th south of Walnut, 4th north of city limits, from Fox to East River.

Quincy street, 6th east of Fox Rriver, from river on north to limits on the south.

School street, short street, north side of Jackson square.

Spring Street, short street, north side of Webster square, between Madison and Monroe.

St. Claire street, north of and parallel to bend in East River, between Eleventh and Twelfth streets.

10

St. George street, 1st east of East River, and extends from
city limits on north, to East River on south, intersecting
Cedar and Main streets.

Stuart street, 2d south of Walnut, east from Fox River to
city limits, and intercepted by Jackson square.

Suydam street, 12th north of Fox River on Emilie.

Twelfth street, 12th north of Fox River, extends from
river on north to limits on south.

Van Buren street, 8th east of Fox River.

Washington street, 1st north of Fox River, extends from
river on north, to intersection of Adams.

Webster, 9th east of Fox River.

Willow, 6th north of Walnut, 3d north of Main, extends
from river west to Jefferson east.

GREEN BAY

City Directory.

1874-5.

ABBREVIATIONS USED IN THIS DIRECTORY.

av., avenue.	N. or n., north.	st., street.
bet., between.	ne., northeast.	S. or s., south.
bds., boards.	n. s., north side.	sc., southeast.
bld., building.	nw., northwest.	s. s., south side.
blk., block.	opp., opposite.	sw., southwest.
cor., corner.	rd., road.	W. or w., west.
E. or e., east.	res., residence.	w. s., west side.
e. s. east side.	Rev. Reverend.	wid., widow.
nr., near	sq., square.	wks., works.

The classification by business will be found immediately after the alphabetical arrangement of names. For full indices to the contents of the work, and names too too late for regular insertion, see preceding pages.

A

Abbott, Mrs M B, wid, res No 239 Jefferson

Abrams, W J, Sec G B and M R R, Shaylor blk, res se cor Crooks and Webster

Achenbrerner, John, shoemaker, res s s of Elm, 3d e St. George

Achenbrerner, Mike, cigar maker, res s s Elm, 3d e St. George

Ackerman, B, carpenter, res s s Cass, 1st w of Eleventh.

Ackerman, Miss E, seamstress, 145 Washington

Ackerman, Geo, pattern maker, res n s of Pine, 3d e of Clay

Adams House, W S Adams, 1st n of Cherry

Adams, Samuel, barkeeper, 114 Washington
Addison, Albert, res se cor Madison and Willow
Addison, Geo, teamster, 120 Washington, res se cor Madison and Willow
Addison, W, cooper, shop and res se cor Madison and Willow
Agry, David, probate judge, bds ne cor Cherry and Jackson
AHRBERG, C, grocer, No 154 Washington, res No 185 Pine
Aird, H, stationary engineer, res ne cor Jefferson and Elm
Alargnon, Peter, laborer, res n s of Cass, 1st w of Twelfth
Albertson, A, cabinet-maker, works for W H Marvin
Albright, H H, res w s of Webster, 2d s of Crooks
Alden, Chas, grocer and dry-goods, store on Main nr bridge, res 221 Main st
Alden, S W, wood dealer, res 225 Main st
Aldhoff, Henry, cabinet-maker, res n s of Walnut, 3d e of Quincy
Aldrich, Wm, R R conductor, res sw cor Crooks and Jackson
Aldrich, Wm, cooper, res 221 Main st
Allen, Frank, watchman, res 376 Walnut
Allen, Fred, painter, bds s s of Walnut, 5th w of Adams
Alston, Gabe, ostler, Fox River House
Alton, Jas T, civil engineer, G B and M R R, res w s of Webster, 1st n of Crooks
Althoff, Kate, No 40 Pine st
Alves, Louis, tanner, bds n s of Main, 3d w of Twelfth
American Express Co, office Shaylor blk
Anderson, Andrew, baker, No 40 Pine st
Anderson Andrew, turner, bds at Minnesota House
Anderson, Beta, laundress at steam laundry
Anderson, Hans, teamster, bds 239 Main
Anderson, Jos, fisherman, res n s of Cherry, 4th e of Twelfth
Anderson, Ole, carpenter, bds United States Hotel
Andræ, L, furnaceman, res w s of Twelfth, 2d n of Elm
Anger, William, laborer, res ne cor Walnut and Monroe
Anhauser, Peter, clerk, res s s of Main, 2d w of Jackson
Anhauser, P J, grocer, s s of Main, 2d west of Jackson
ANSORGE, E K, insurance agt, 103 Washington, res e s Monroe, 3d s of Doty
Antoinan, Jos, laborer, res n s of Pine, 1st e of Clay
Arends, F, clerk, No 121 Washington, bds w s of St George, 1st n of Elm
Armitage, G D, job printer Advocate office, res e s of Quincy, 2d n of Doty
Armstrong, John, laborer, res 187 Walnut
Armstrong, Rob't, drayman, res s s Doty, 2d w of Clay
Armstrong, Wm, laborer, s s Lawe, 1st e of Jefferson

Arter, Theodore, stave shipper, res s s Pine, 2d w of Jackson
Arthur, Mary, laundress, res rear of Shaylor blk
Aschenbach, Benj, laborer, res w s of Monroe, 1st n of Grignon
Aschenbrenner J, Jr., printer, Volkszeitung office
Ashton, ——, bds 221 Adams
Asimond, S, apprentice, No. 147 Washington
Asimont, E, jeweler, 177 Washington
Asimont, H, painter, bds 177 Washington
Asimont, Mrs J, wid, No 177 Washington st
Ast, Chas, painter, res w s of Jackson, 2d s of Walnut
Astor Engine Co, Astor Place
Astor Mills, cor Washington and Doty
Astor Place, intersection of Washington and Adams
Astor Saloon cor Washington and Chicago sts
Atkinson, Miss Bridget, compositor, Gazette office, res Ft Howard
Atkinson, H, res No 12 Quincy
Atkinson, John, drayman, No 66 Quincy
Atwood, A J, lumber dealer, Shaylor's blk, bds Adams House
Atwood, Dan G, freight ag't, G B and M R R
Atwood, S, laborer, bds 275 Main
Aubol, Annie, 260 Jefferson
Auction and Commission, 77 Washington
AVERY, C S, (G N Langton & Co,) flour and feed, 106 Washington, res ne cor Cherry and Jackson
Averill, Rev M V, res No 101 Cherry
Ayers, Burley, clerk, 122 Washington, (2d story,) bds sw cor Washington and Crooks
AYERS, D C, physician and surgeon, 149 Washington, res se cor VanBuren and Pine sts

B

Bacon, J B, travelling salesman, 237 Adams
Bacon, E H, salesman, 92 Washington, res 182 Mason
Bacon, H, wholesale grocer, 92 Washington, res 182 Mason
Bacon, S, tailor, 111 Washington, res Ft Howard
Baendwin, Peter, mason, res n s Main, 2d e VanBuren
Baenen, John, carpenter, res w s of Monroe, 2d s of Grignon
Baier; Frank, east river brewery, bds the same
BAILEY, W C, attorney over First National Bank, res se cor Crooks and Jackson
Bailey, Ellen, waitress, Beaumont House
Baird, H S, attorney's office and res, No 139 Main st

Baker, Elizabeth, 149 Cherry st
Baker, H B, book-keeper, Kellogg National Bank, res 132 Main
BAKER, J S, land ag't, 31 Pine, res 132 Main
Baker, Max, ostler, Green Bay House
Balt, Christ, res No 299 Main st
Baltee, Chas, tinsmith, bds United States Hotel
Bannister, H D, superintendent gas works, res e s of Jefferson, 1st s of Main
Banx, H, clerk, res ne cor Main and Adams
Barber, Sarah, n s Walnut, 2d e of bridge
Barchansen, Henry, clerk, 119 Washington, bds e s of Jefferson, 2d s of Pine
Bardelme, Kate, e s VanBuren, 1st n Emilie
Bardouch, P, painter, res e s of Jacksou, 1st s of Doty
Bardouch, T B, teamster, res n s Elm, 2d e of Madison
Barker, E L, carpenter, res No 258 Cherry st
Barkowerk, P, tanner, res n s Stuart, 1st w of Eleventh
Bartmas, F, grocer, n s Crooks, 1st e of Eleventh
Barnard, Frank, cooper, res n s Cedar, 3d w of Monroe
Barnes, Mrs Arlette, wid, res sw cor Crooks and Washington
Barnson, Henry, laborer, res w s Quincy, 2d s of Crooks
Barso, Seymour, carpenter, res w s Twelfth, 2d n of Willow
Barth, A, liquor dealer, No 42 Pine st, res w s of Madison, 3d s of Walnut
Bartholma, Louis, proprietor of saloon, 112 Washington, res e s of Quincy, 1st s of Chicago
Basche, Anthony, shoe dealer, cor Pine and Washington, res 297 Cedar
Basche, Fred W, notion dealer, cor of Cherry and Adams, res ne cor of Jefferson and Mason
Basche, M, carpenter, res e s Jefferson, 2d n of Mason
Bassel, John, laborer, bds s s Chicago, 1st e of Eleventh
Bassett, Stephen, laborer, res se cor Eleventh and Cedar st
Bast, Martin, laborer, res s s of Pine, 2d e of Clay
Basten, F. J, res e end of Main st
Basten, James, propr Three Corner House, e end of Main st
Batiska, John, mason, res 336 Cedar st
Bauer, John, tanner, bds n s of Main, 3d w of Twelfth
Bay, Campbell, stage driver, bds United States Hotel
Bay City House, cor Washington and Walnut
Bazizore, Peter, peddler, res No 305 Cedar st
Beans, Jacob, laborer, res, s s Stuart, last house east
BEARD, L F, insurance ag't, post office blk, res nw cor Jefferson and Doty
Beats, John, laborer, res w s VanBuren, 1st n of Doty

Beaupre, W, proprietor of saloon, s s of Main, 5th w of
Adams, res w s Quincy, 2d n of Mason
Beaulieu, Eli, clerk, bds ne cor Jefferson and Milwaukee
Beauchamp, Julius, boot and shoe dealer, 49 Cherry,
Beauchamp, G, boot and shoe dealer, 49 Cherry
Beaumont House, ne cor Main and Washington
Beaumont, J C, res 225 Jefferson
Beaver, A, laborer, res n e cor Pine and Eleventh, (2d story)
Befay, Dennis, clerk, 84 Washington, res n s Stuart, 3d w of
Twelfth
Bernson, John, brick-maker, res s s of Main, 1st w of Web-
ster
Bender, D, laborer, res w s of Monroe, 4th s of Walnut
Bender, Elizabeth, wid, res s s of Walnut, 2d w of Jackson
Bender, Geo, saw setter, res n s of Cedar, 2d e of Jefferson
Bender, Louis, proprietor of saloon, e s of Washington, 2 s
of Walnut, res w s of Monroe, 4th s of Walnut
Bengley, N, clerk, 118 Washington, bds 124 Walnut
Benjamin, A C, foreman in lumber mill, res w s VanBuren,
1st s of Doty
Benjamin, S A, shingle cutter, res ne cor of VanBuren and
Doty
Bennett, L M, salesman 113 Washington, res No 174 Cherry
Bennett, Thos, ice merchant, res 310 Adams
Beno, Florent, proprietor of saloon and boarding, Main nr
Adams, res s s of Walnut, 2d e of Quincy
Bennon, Henry, carpenter, res w s of Webster, 2d n of Doty
BENSON, M V B, insurance ag't office over First National
Bank, res s w corner of Crooks and Monroe
Benz, Cassimer, clerk, 109 Washington, res No 181 Cherry
Berendsen, B, proprietor of Astor Saloon, cor of Washing-
ton and Chicago
Berendt, Chas, laborer, res w s of Jackson, 2d s of Gringon
Berner, Chas, grocer, 119 Washington, res e s of Jefferson,
2d s of Pine
Berond, Stephen, carpenter, bds s s of Chicago, 1st e of Clay
BERTLES, J F, engineer of fire engine No 1, res 179 Wash-
ington
Bertman Virginia, laundress, Beaumont House
BEST, T L, merchant, 127 Washington, res nw cor of Pine
and Jackson
Bester, Frank, saloon, s s of Main, 1st e of Clay
BETH, JOHN, potter, 81 Washington, res s s of Walnut, 3d e
of Twelfth.
Bews, Geo, painter, office cor Pine and Washington
Bey, Phebe, wid, n s stuart, 1st w of Eleventh

11

Beyers, M, brewer, res nw cor Chicago and Jackson
Biemeret, G, east river brewery, bds same
Biemeret, P G, laborer, res s s Cherry, 3d e of Clay
Bienner, Chas, ostler, cor Washington and Walnut, bds 44
    Walnut
BILLINGS, L J, attorney, nw cor Pine and Adams, res w s of
    Quincy, 3d s of Chicago
Bingham, T B, supply clerk, Green Bay and M R R office,
    rooms the same
Bingley, ——, clerk, 118 Washington, bds 124 Walnut
Bins, Lizzie, e s of Jefferson, 2d s of Walnut
Bisbee, D W F, res s e cor Chicago aud VanBuren
Bissner, Mike, bds at Fox River House
Blackman, A C, principal Green Bay Business College, No
    153 Washington
Blaser, Elizabeth, No 48 Walnut
Bleidung, Carl, druggist, 29 Cherry, res the same
Blein, Miss Maggie, dress maker, No 13 Quincy
Blesch, Andrew, proprietor of restaurant, 201 Main
Bleischke, Christian, laborer, res w s of Cass, 3d n of
    Eleventh
Blochoveak, Franz, furnaceman, res s s of Stuart, 3d e of
    Twelfth
Blumberg, Amos, carpenter, res sw cor of Walnut and
    Twelfth
Blumberg, Mrs Ida, hair-maker, No 148 Washington
Boaler, Edwin, 403 and 405 Main st, res the same
Bock, F, teamster, res w s of Washington, 2d s of Crooks
Bodart, Euphrasia, Waterloo House
Bodart House, n s of Main, bet Adams and Jefferson
Bodart, Henry, laborer, res Bodart House
Bodart, W, proprietor of Bodart House, also clothier s s of
    Main 4th east of Adams
BODLE, D W, proprietor Adams House
Bogart, Mrs Archer, w s Adams, 3d s of Walnut
Bohemian Aid and Educational Society, rooms 84 Main
Bohl, Mrs M T, wid, res s s Chicago, 2d e of Eleventh
Boluvka, Frank, laborer, res e s St George, 2d n of Elm
Boland, E P, clerk, 64 and 70 Washington, res Ft Howard
Bombarnes, Isadore, laborer, res 365 Walnut
Bombers, Egils, laborer, res 315 Jefferson
Bombers, Jos, clerk, res 315 Jefferson
Boncha, Jos, plasterer, res n s Stuart, 4th e of Eleventh
Bond, ——, bds 221 Adams
Bonerfiend, Ernest, carpenter, res e s of Jackson, 2d n of Stuart

Boness, William, harness-maker, res n s of Doty, 3d w of
Twelfth
Bong, Gerhard, policeman, res se cor Quincy and Stuart
Bongie, Stephen, blacksmith, on Main, res e s of Quincy, 2d
s of Chicago
Bonneville, Alfred, lumberman, res sw cor Walnut and
Webster
Boomer, Ed, res s s of Main, 5th w of Adams
Bordon, Miss, teacher, bds 262 Adams
Borth, Jos, res w s Madison, 3d s of Walnut
Boughton, O S, clerk, 120 Washington, res 273 Adams
Boulet, C J, teamster, 119 Washington, res n s Main, 1 w of
Adams, (2d story)
Bourne, Capt Wm R, res e s VanBuren, 2d s of Mason
Bouzie, S, carriage maker, 1st e of City Hotel
Boxy, L. hatter, store and res w s of Adams, 2d n of Pine
Boyd, Edward, laborer, res No 305 Cedar
Boyle, Nellie, waitress, Beaumont House
Braasch, C, veterinary surgeon, res s s of Main, 5th e of Clay
Brabant, Mary, res w s of Madison, 1st s of Cedar
Bracken, Geo R, sailor, res w s of Quincy, 3d s of Crooks
Bradle, Jos, laborer, bds n s of Main, 3 e of Twelfth
Bradley, Dan'l, teamster, Joannes Bros, res n s of Crooks, 1st
e of Monroe
Brady, Kitty, n s Walnut, 2d e of bridge
Braehchl, Henry, proprietor east river tannery
Brandenstein, W A, tailor shop and res s s of Walnut, 3d w
o l Jackson
Brandenstein, W A, tailor, 25 Cherry st
Brandt, Aug, furnaceman, res s s of Doty, 3d e of Twelfth
Brandt, Chas, hack-driver, res e s of Quincy, 2d n of Stuart
Brannen, Bridget, w s Madison, 4th s of Stuart
Brauns, Aug, grocer, 174 and 176 Washington, res 283 Adams
Brawski, John, furnaceman, res s s Doty, 4th e of Twelfth
Brennan, J, proprietor head quarters saloon, No 114 Wash-
ington
Brennan, J, clerk, 136 Washington
Brennon, Mary A, e s Monroe, 3d s of Crooks
Bresnahn, Miss Johanna, dress-maker, w s of Quincy, 3d s of
Crooks
Brett. Dr B C, office Fox's blk, res e s Monroe, 3d s of
Crooks
Brett, Jas, painter, bds s s of Cass, 2d e of Adams
Brice, Geo, painter, bds No 202 Walnut st
BRICE, O J B, notary, office ne cor Main and Adams, res s s
of Cherry, 2d w of Clay

Bricknier, John, apprentice, No 29 Pine st
Bridgman, W J, express messenger, C and N W R R, bds National Hotel
Briece, A, furniture, s s Main, 4th e of Adams, res s s Walnut, 2d e of Webster
Briece, L, furniture, s s Main, 4th e of Adams, res s s of Walnut, 2d e of Webster
Brien, T N, boot and shoe dealer, 49 Cherry, res w s Adams, 2d s of Cherry
Brien, L, boot and shoe dealer, 44 Cherry, res w s Adams, 2d s of Cherry
BRIGGS, L W, principal of high school, res w s Morrison 2d n of Cherry
Bringham, Chas E, sailor, res e s of Quincy, 1st n of Stuart
Briot, Chas, clerk, post office, res s s Cedar, 1st w of Jefferson
Briot, Eugene, painter, res s s Cedar, 1st w of Jefferson
Briquelett, J, liquor dealer, 149 Washington, res Shanty Town
Briskiel, J A, clerk, Fox River House
Britton, Andrew, carpenter, res 42 Doty
Britton, Mrs A J, proprietor city laundry, No 42 Doty
Brooks, H E, ship builder, res s s of Walnut, 6th e of Clay
Brooks, J A, lake captain, res s s Walnut, 6th e of Clay
Brought, John W, contractor, res s s of Doty, 1st e of Adams
Brown, Barbara, servant, e s Adams, 1st n of Doty
Brown, Chas N, res e s Jefferson, 2d s of Cass
Brown, Dan'l C, commission merchant, rear of 74 Washington, res 347 Jefferson
Brown, Mrs F A, wid, res e s Quincy, 2d n of Walnut
Brown, F L, printer, res 326 Jefferson
Brown, H F, 326 Jefferson
Brown, H O, clerk, 74 Washington, bds s s Walnut, 2d w of Webster
Brown, J, saddler, No 144 Washington
Brown, Miss Kate, res n s Stuart, 5th e of Clay
Brown, Mrs L R, wid, res e s Jefferson, 2d s of Cass
Brown, Mrs Mary, wid, res No 139 Walnut
Brown, Miss Mary A, seamstress, bds ne cor of Adams and Brooks
Brown, Peter, bar keeper, New York saloon, res s s Pine, 1st e of Jackson
Brown, Sam'l A, tinner, res w s Jackson, 2d n of Cass
Brown, S C, mason, res n s Walnut, 2d w of Twelfth
Brown, S C, express messenger, bds 221 Adams
Brown, P W, carpenter, res n s Walnut, 8th e of Twelfth
Brugere, Aug, clerk, (VanNostrand, Klause & Co)

Brugere, Leopold, blacksmith, res s s Cedar, 3d e of St George
Brugere, Jos, laborer, res 248 Cherry
Brulette, W, barber for J Dufresne, cor Pine and Adams
Burnett, Peter, carpenter, res e s Jefferson, 2d s of Mason
Brunnar, Jos, blacksmith, res n s Cedar, 3d e of St George
Bruno, Wm, stage driver, bds United States Hotel
Bublitz, Aug, tanner, res s s of Willow, 1st e of Twelfth
Bublitz, Bertha, nw cor of Stuart and Twelfth
Bublitz, Herman, tailor, res n s of Doty, 3d e of Eleventh
Bucher, Louis, teamster, res e s Jefferson, 2d n of Elm
Budd, E R, land-surveyor, res n s Cedar, 1st w of Quincy
Buengener, Aug, clerk, 119 Washington, bds e s Jefferson, 2d s of Pine
Buirnt, John, laborer, res No 177 Cherry st
Bulgick, Frank, laborer, bds e s VanBuren, 2d n of Doty
Bumber, Henry, laborer, res s s Cherry, 5th e of Twelfth
Buncher, Louisa, ne cor Walnut and Webster
Bur, Maria, e s Adams, 3d n of Doty
Burger, John B, tailor, res 372 Cherry
Burghardt, F, butcher, No 158 Washington, res the same
Burgin, O H, clerk, bds 221 Adams
Burk, Jas, laborer, res e s Washington, 2d s of Stuart
Burk, Patrick, mason, bds s s Cass, 2d e of Adams
BURKART, ANTON, furniture, 41 Cherry, res se cor Cherry and Jackson
BURKART, ANTON, JR, furniture, s s Main 3d w of Jefferson, res cor St George and Doty
Burkard, Fred, painter, res n s Cherry, 1st w of Webster
Burkard, Milo, machinist, res nw cor Jackson and Stuart
Burkard, V, printer, Wis Staats Zeitung, res s s Doty, 1st e of Clay
Burkhardt, Rosa, w s Jefferson, 2d n of Crooks
Burke, J, res w s of Adams, 2d s of Cass
Burmeas, Wm, laborer, res n s Polier, 1st e of Twelfth
Burns, Jas, bummer, bds at United States Hotel
Burns, Thos, painter, res s s Cherry, 2d w of VanBuren
BUSCHER, J, proprietor of steam dye works, Washington bet Doty and Crooks
Busch, ——, butcher, e s Adams, 1st n of Pine
Bushle, Rev Father A N, priest, res ne cor Madison & Doty
BUTLER, DAN'L, merchant, 91 Washington, res 203 Adams
BUTLER, W S, merchant, 91 Washington, res 203 Adams
Button, D W, wooden ware manufacturer, res No 174 Washington
Buttrick, A, laborer, res se cor Cass and Clay

C

Cable, Jos, painter for M F Lampson, bds s s Walnut, 5th w of Adams

Cadle Home, w s of Madison, 1st s of Pine

Calhoun Square, s s of Crooks, bet Jefferson and Madison

Call, Chas C, sailor, res 289 Main

Call Ranson, fish packer, res 289 Main

Call, T W, contractor, res 216 Pine

Calyer, Dan, laborer, 92 Washington, bds at restaurant

Cameron, Will M, book-keeper, 36 Pine, bds 267 Adams

Can John, res n s Cedar, 3d e St George

Canghman, John, drayman, res n s Main, 3d w of Jackson

Cannon, H, section boss, C & N W R R, bds e s Washington, 4th s of Stuart

Carabin, Mrs, Ellen, wid, res ne cor Crooks and Jefferson

Carabin, Louis, Green Bay gas works, res ne cor Crooks and Jefferson

Carbeno, Louis, bds at United States Hotel

Cardinal, Jos, millwright, res 336 Walnut

Carney, Mary, dining room, Fox River House

Caron, Ambrose, perfumer, No 76 Washington

Caron, Miss A, shirt and dress-maker, No 76 Washington

Carpenter, W B, grocer, No 128 Washington, bds 124 Walnut

Carpenter B, sewing machine ag't, 78 Washington

Carswell, Walter, grocer, 162 Washington, res se cor Monroe and Stuart

Case, C E, merchant, 64, 66, 68, and 70 Washington, res s s Walnut, 2d e of Madison

Case, John H, clerk, 155 Washington, bds 221 Adams

Caston, Mich, blacksmith, cor Washington and Doty, bds e s Washington, 3d s of Stuart

Catlin, A P, commercial traveler, res 275 Adams

Catlin, E A, painter for M F Lampson, bds s s Walnut, 5th w of Adams

CATLIN, COL T B, painter, 96 Washington, res n s Stuart, 2d e of Adams

Catmel, Bella, No 132 Main

Cauly, Edward, furnaceman, res n s Main, 3d w of Jackson

Cauwenberghs, J B, grocer, No 34 Main, res the same

Cawthorne, W B, pedlar, res e s Madison, 4th s of Crooks

Cazean, F F, clerk, res e s Quincy, 2d n of Stuart

Cent, Peter, tailor, res s s Mason, 2d w of Madison

Central Baptist Church, cor Madison and Moravian sts

Chaeve, John, laborer, res n s Main, 4th w of VanBuren

Chaeve, Mrs Lena, milliner, res n s Main 4th w of VanBuren

21

Chaffee, Mrs Anna, plain sewing, 98 Washington, 2d floor
Chaffee, C, breaksman, C & N W R R, bds Fox River
  House
Chapman, C F, meat-cutter, s s Cherry, bet Washington and
  Adams, res w s Adams, 2d s of Cherry
Chapman, H W, res 285 Adams
Chapman, Wm Col, res 211 Adams
Chartrand, Paul, wagon-maker, n s Main, bet Clay and
  Eleventh, res 367 Main
Charwat, Jos, shoemaker, n s Walnut, 3d s of bridge, res
  Prebil
Chase, Miss Eva S, bds 147 Monroe
Chavet, Maggie, ne cor Quincy and Crooks
Chepek, John, east river brewery
Cherot, C R, clerk, 117 Washington, res w s Quincy, 4th n
  of Chicago
Cherot, Miss Elmira, res e s Monroe, 3d s of Stuart
Cherot, Leonce, Druggist, 117 Washington, res e s Monroe,
  3d s of Stuart
Chevet, Julius, laborer, res n s Stuart, 2d W of Eleventh
Chon, Matilda, res e s of VanBuren, 2d s of Main
Choynowski, M, carpenter, res se cor Walnut and Eleventh
Christ Church P E, nw cor Cherry and Madison
Christains, Martin, blacksmith, res nw cor Cedar and
  Eleventh
Christains, Peter, laborer, w s VanBuren, 1st n of Emily
Christianson, Annie, No 162 Jefferson
Christman, Antoine, carpenter, res ne cor Clay and Cherry
Christman, Jacob, painter, res nw cor Walnut and Webster
Christian, John, drayman, res nw cor Walnut and Webster
Chueller, John, apprentice, bds e s Jackson, 2d n of Crooks
Chunck, Chas, saloon, Washington, res ne cor Quincy and
  Walnut
Chynoweth, T B, attorney, Shaylor Blk, bds Beaumont
  House
City brewery, sw cor Chicago and Jackson, Landwehr &
  Beyer, proprietors
City Hotel, cor Washington and Walnut
Clark, C A, res w s VanBuren, 2d s of Cherry
Clark, Daniel, carpenter, bds 275 Main
Clark, D, bds First National Hotel
Clark, E L, baggageman, G B & M R R, bds 267 Adams
Clary, Thos, laborer, bds No 13 Quincy
Clausson, Mrs, milliner, 70 Washington, room No 1
Clement, Albert, teamster, res w s St George, 1st n of
  Cedar.

Cleveland, Chas L, carpenter, res s s Cherry, 7th e of Twelfth

Clifford, Kate, waitress, Beaumont House

Clintsman, H, dry goods salesman, res c s Washington, 4th s of Walnut

Clossen, Ike, ostler at Hagens livery, bds at Adams House

Clough, Cornelius, watchman, res No 89 Cedar

Cluff, H M, s s Main, 4th w of Adams, 2d floor

Cluff, Frank, marble cutter, Green Bay marble works

Codding, J, sailor, res ne cor Cedar and Quincy

COEL, F, proprietor Waterloo House, n s Main, bet Adams and Jefferson

Cohen, Henry, merchant, bds 221 Adams

Cohen, L, merchant, cor Adams and Walnut

Cohen, R, merchant, cor Adams and Walnut

Cointe, A, blacksmith, c s of Adams, 2d s of Main, res w s of Adams, 2d s of Main

Colburn, Mrs N, wid, res 200 Jackson

Coleman, Albert, res ne cor Cherry and Webster

Coleman, M, laborer, res 270 Walnut st

Coller, V, carpenter, res n s Willow, on city limits

Colwell, John, sailor, res 275 Main

Combes, John, French teacher, res 281 Stuart

Compman, John, laborer, res 251 Crooks

Conery, Mrs S E, seamstress, res c s Adams, 2d n of Chicago

Conner, Frank, laborer, res 78 Elm

Conner, Miss P, dress maker, No 45 Cherry

Connup, Mary, 216 Pine

Cook, C, proprietor Minnesota House, n s of Main, bet Adams and Jefferson

Cook, Geo R, shingle manufacturer, res 283 Monroe

Cook, Jas, clerk, se cor Washington and Main, res with R W Cook

Cook, R W, grocer, se cor Washington and Main, res c s Adams, 1st n of Main

Cook, Mrs Rose, wid, res e s Adams, 1st n of Main

Coppersmith, D, stone cutter, res 250 Quincy

Cooper, Frank, laborer, bds s s Cedar, 3d w of VanBuren

Cooper, J, laborer, bds w s Jefferson, 4th s of Mason

COREY, W C, dentist, 140 Washington, res ne cor Madison and Chicago

CORMIER, D, JR, liquor dealer, 136 Washington, res w s Jackson, 1st n of Mason

Cornell, Jas Sr, cooper, res n s Cherry, 5th e of Twelfth

Cornell, Jas Jr, cooper, res n s Cherry, 5th e of Twelfth

Corning, Cyrus, attorney, res e s Webster, 3d s of Doty

Correa, John, book-keeper, First National Bank
Corrigan, T B, res es Monroe, 1st n of Crooks
Corty, John, laborer, res nw cor Chicago and Adams
Cotte, John, laborer, res Astor saloon building .
Cottrell, John, shoemaker, 129 Washington
Cotton, Mrs C H, wid, res 226 Jefferson
Cotton, Geo H, book-keeper, res 226 Jefferson
Copei, A, salesman, 80 Washington
Coulter, Geo, stationary engineer, res e s Quincy, 3d s of
    Crooks
Couch, Tom, (col,) Hagens ommibus barn, rear of Beaumont
Council Rooms over post-office
COZZENS, ALFRED, proprietor Beaumont House
COZZENS, M F, proprietor Beaumont House
Cramer, Albert, laborer, res 317 Pine
Crandall, D S, printer, Gazette office, bds e s Monroe, 3d n of
    Walnut
Crandall, W I, grocer, 32 and 34 Pine, res w s Jefferson, 2d n
    of Crooks
Crane, Chas E, city mayor
Cranny, Jas T, auctioneer, res nw cor Jackson and Stuart
Crawford, Rev W, res sw cor Crooks and Adams
Creager, Augusta, res sw cor Monroe and Crooks
Creager, Fred, laborer, res n s Doty, 4th e of Eleventh
Cressler, Jacob, engineer, res No 394 Cherry
CRIKELAIR, FRANK, painter, e s Adams, 2d s of Cherry,
    bds w s Adams, 3d s of Cherry
Crikelair, Gustave. proprietor bowling saloon, w s Adams,
    3d s of Cherry
Cripling, Wm, tinner, res No 189 Walnut
Cronan, M, turner, bds Minnesota House
Crosby, Fred, painter, bds 48 Walnut.
Cull, John, teamster, res w s Jackson, 3d n of Crooks
Crud, Rev P H, Pastor of St John's, res next e of church,
    w s Milwaukee st
Cunna, Mike, laborer, bds e s VanBuren, 2d n of Doty
Currier, A, carpenter, bds Fox River House
Currier, J W, painter, bds s s Walnut, 5th w of Adams
Curtin, David, assistant cashier, National Bank of Commerce
    res e s of Madison, 2d n of Chicago
Curtis, Anton, laborer, res s s Cherry, 1st w of Twelfth
Curtis, J, attorney, cor Pine and Adams, res s s Grignon,
    bet Jackson and VanBuren
Custom House, Post-office building, w s Adams, bet Pine and
    Cherry

D

Dagnean, J J, barkeeper at Waterloo House
Dalle, Henry, teamster, res n s Cherry, 3d e of Eleventh
Dallinger, Barton, mason, res n s Cedar, 1st w of Quincy
Danbach, Andrew, laborer, res n s Cherry, 3d w of Twelfth
Dandoiz, Frank, saloon keeper, res w s Webster, 3d n of Doty
Daniel, Mathias, laborer, res n s Crooks, 4th e of Clay
Danz, Herman, tinner, res 193 Walnut
Danz, John B, tailor, res se cor Pine and Quincy
Darby, C, phonographer, G B & M R R, bds ne cor Cherry
    and Jefferson
Darigan, Thos, laborer, res n s Cass, 1st e of Clay
Darwin, David, penman, res 344 Main
Darwin, John, wagon-maker, n s Cedar, 1st w of Jackson,
    res 344 Main
Darwin, Peter, carpenter, res 344 Main
Dashley, Henry, laborer, res s s Mason, 1st e of Clay
Davidson, Otto, messenger First National Bank
Davis, A L, cook, Beaumont House
Daugherty, Jas, tinsmith, bds Fox River House
DAY, L J, wholesale grocer, 92 Washington, res nw cor
    Madison and Lawe
Day, Maggie, cook, Fox River House
Daybien, John, laborer, res w s Baird, 1st s of Cass
Deall, Louis, teamster, res 397 Adams
Debrion, John, laborer, res n s Elm, 3d e St George
Debrue, D, tailor, res n s Elm, 3d e of Twelfth
DECKER, E, banker, National Bank of Commerce, res e s
    Madison, 2d n of Chicago
Decremer, Chas, clerk, 128 Washington, res n s Pine, 1st e of
    Webster
Decremer, F, flour and feed, 79 washington, res n s Pine, 2d
    w of Quincy
DeGreef, Jos, janitor, G B & M Railroad offices
DeHie, Andrew, furnaceman, bds w s Jackson, 2d n of Doty
Deisch, Jos, saloon and res, 355 Main
DeKeizer, Frank, laborer, res 320 Jefferson
DeKeizer, Mrs Mary, wid, res 320 Jefferson
DeKelven, Frank, carpenter, res w s VanBuren 2d n Crooks
DeKelven, Peter, carpenter, res w s VanBuren, 2d n Crooks
Delacenserie, E, watchman, res w s Quincy, 2d s of Stuart
Delaporte, L, hardware, 87 Washington, res n s Walnut, 1st
    w of Quincy
Delaporte, C, clothier, 137 Washington, res the same

Delasenserie, Emil, baggage master, W C R R, res w s Quincy, 2d s of Stuart

Delforge, Aug, proprietor East River foundry, res 326 Main

Delforge, Frank, machinist, res s s Main, 3d w of Clay

Delgofle, Aug, proprietor Tremont House, cor Main and Twelfth

Delgofle, Wm, blacksmith, res se cor Main and Twelfth

Dellingre, Frank, res sw cor Elm and Twelfth

Dellvage, A, laborer, res e s Jefferson, 2d s of Willow

DeLong, Jos, clothes, cleaner, e end of Walnut st bridge

Delwiche, W, saloon, s s Main, 3d e of Cherry, res 224 Cherry

Demers, Jos, wagon maker, res n s Main, 3d e of Clay

Dempsey, Dan'l, laborer, res s s Chicago, 1st e of Clay

Dempske, Thos, carpenter, bds s s Chicago, 1st e of Twelfth

Denamur, Jos, laborer, bds at Waterloo House

Dene, F, furnaceman, res n s Cedar, 3d e of Twelfth

Denemere, Philippine, bds Waterloo House

Denlear, Julia, res nw cor Jefferson and Chicago

Denning, Mike, laborer, bds United States Hotel

Dennis, H, w s Adams, 3d s of Cherry

DENNIS, JOHN ST, proprietor steam laundry, w s Washington, 3d s of Crooks

Dennis, Josh, lake captain, res e s VanBuren, 1st n of Crooks

Dennis, Louis, engineer of steamer No 2, bds 47 Main

Depra, Frank, laborer, res s s Cedar, 4th e of Clay

DeQuindre, Mrs Susan, wid, res 206 Adams

Derby, ——, clerk, bds ne cor Cherry and Jefferson

Deese, Matilda, laundress, Beaumont House

Deidrich, Carl, proprietor steam laundry, bds nw cor Quincy and Jackson

Derwae, A C, grocery and res e s Jefferson, 4th s of Mason

Desers, Mary, laundress, steam laundry

Detienne, J P, clerk at post office

Detienne, V, painter, bds w s Adams, 3d s of Cherry

Detry, E, tailor, res ne cor Walnut and Clay sts

Detterer, Rev J J, res s s Moravian, 2d e of Madison

Deuster, Jas, miller, res sw cor Doty and Twelfth

Deuster, John, miller, res sw cor Doty and Twelfth

Deuster, Louis, miller, res sw cor Doty and Twelfth

Devroey, Dan'l, grocer, sw cor Main and Adams, bds Green Bay House

Dewitt, Francis, laborer, res s s Crooks, 2d e of Eleventh

Dexhenenmont, ——, tailor, s s Main, 4th e of Adams

Dhyne, Jos, res n s of Mason, 1st w of Eleventh

Dickensen, C M, general ag't Davis Sewing machine Co, res 224 Madison

Dickensen, E W, meat-cutter, res e s Adams, 3d n of Pine
Dickensen, E W, butcher, s s of Cherry, 5th e of Fox River House
Dickson, Wm, cook, res n s Cherry, 2d e of Twelfth
Dickman, F A, salesman, 149 Washington, bds Whitney House
Dietz, Mike, painter, res w s of Twelfth, 1st n of Elm
Dimerer, Mary, servant, w s VanBuren, 1st n Emilie
Dittmer, L, shoemaker, w s Adams, 1st n of Pine
Dittmer, W, shoemaker, shop and res s s Main, 2d e of Webster
Dlirulle, Herbert, shingle sawyer, res n s Walnut, 3d w of Eleventh
Dohoney, J, barber, 47 Cherry
Dolan, E, bds at St Louis House
Doncy, W T, cooper, res se cor Madison and Willow
Donville, H B, boot and shoe dealer, cor Pine and Washington, res s s Main, 1st w of Monroe
Doty, Miss Emma, compositor, Gazette office, res Ft Howard
Doty, Solomon, carpenter, res 275 Main
Doty, Mrs Margaret, milliner, 148 Washington res the same
Doubleruske, Louis, res s s Cedar, 1st e of Clay
Doublk, Mary, 206 Quincy
DOUSMAN, MISS J, res w s Madison, 1st s of Crooks
DOUGHERTY, B, stave dealer, office Shaylor blk, res ne cor Quincy and Cass
DOUGHFRTY, J, stave dealer, office Shaylor blk, res ne cor Quincy and Cass
Dray, Anton, carpenter, res n s Cedar, 6th e of Twelfth
Dray, Jack, carpenter, res n s Cedar, 5th e of Twelfth
Dray, Mark, shoemaker, res n s Cedar, 5th e of Twelfth
Dressler, Henry, laborer, res n s Crooks, 3d e of Twelfth
Dreyer, H, clerk, bds 263 Adams
Dreutzer, G A, clerk, No 40 Pine
Driech, Mary, Beaumont House
Drive, Mary, 35 Pine st
Drive Dora, 141 Cherry
Drob, John, horse dealer, res 70 Elm
DuBois, J D, express messenger,. C & N W R R
Dubke, Martin, laborer, res s s Chicago, 3d w of Twelfth
Duchateau, Abel, liquor dealer, 94 Washington, res ne cor Pine and Monroe
Dudley, Jas, drug clerk, cor Washington and Walnut
Duchateaur, Antoine, laborer, res sw cor Mason and Goodell

Duchateaur, L A R, liquor dealer, 94 Washington, res ne cor Pine and Monroe
DUFRESNE, J B, barber, cor Pine and Adams, bds First National Hotel
Dulude, A, butcher, ne cor Pine and Adams
Dunlap, James, engineer, res 106 Cedar
DUNLAP, L H, wholesale cigar dealer, Shaylor's blk, res Ft Howard
Dunn, Mrs Mary, 216 Madison
Dunn, Wm, laborer, 295 Monroe
Durochie, Alex, lake captain, res nw cor Jackson and Eliza
Durochie, Mich, steamboat engineer, res w s Jackson, 2d s of Mason
Duvial, C, clerk, 111 Washington, res s s Cherry, 2d w of Monroe

E

Eagen, Jas, tinner, 113 Washington
Eagle, Annie, sw cor Jefferson and Walnut
Earle, G W, express messenger, res 265 Adams
Earle, P I, lumberman, 62 Washington, res 188 Mason
Eams, Cyrus, res 301 Monroe
East River Foundry, n s of Main, 1st w of bridge
Eastman, B R, clerk, C & N W R R, res sw cor Monroe and Polier
EASTMAN, H E, farmer, res sw cor Monroe and Polier
Eckhardt, Oswald, cigar maker, s s Walnut, 1st w of Washington, res n s Quincy, 2d s of Walnut
Ellen, Fred, painter, bds 48 Walnut
Ellis, Mrs B, wid, 168 Jefferson
Ellis, E H, circuit judge, res w s VanBuren, 1st n of Emilie
ELLIS, FRED L, insurance ag't, cor Pine and Adams, res 6 Cherry
Ellis, Minnie, servant, 285 Adams
Ellsworth, A H, dentist, 123 Washington, res 133 Cherry
Emeigh, J D, gas fitting, No 90 Washington, res e s Quincy 2d n of Mason
Engel, Frank, bds ne cor Quincy and Crooks
ENGELS, EDWARD A, grocer store and res sw cor Main and Jefferson
English Baptist Church, se cor Madison and Moravian
English, Mark, res cor Adams
Enoch, Chas, clerk, 64 and 70 Washington, res s s Doty, 29 w of Quincy

Enterprise Steamer No 1, 179, Washington, J F Bertles, engineer
Erdman, A, barber, s s Main, 3d w of Adams, res n s Main, 2d e of Beaumont
Erdmann, Christian, carpenter, res 189 Walnut
Erdmann, F L, carpenter, res cor Jackson and Doty
Erdmann, Rosa, res s s Crooks, 1st w of Madison
Estey, H H, carpenter, res ne cor Adams and Crooks
Estey, Mrs H H, dress-maker, res ne cor Adams and Crooks
Etches, Peter, laborer, s s Crooks, 1st w of Twelfth
Etienne, P J, proprietor French bakery, store and res s s Pine, 3d e of Adams
Eugine, F, laborer, res s s Cedar, 4th e of Clay
Evans, R C, lumber-dealer, 62 Washington, res e cor Madison and Crooks
Everets, J, laborer gas works, res n s Elm, 2d w of Madison
Everets, J B, boarding, 239 Main

F

Farnsworth, G P, R R contractor, res 214 Cherry
Farr, Mary, milliner, bds at Fox River House
Farron, Frank, cattle dealer, res nw cor Crooks and Eleventh
Fassal, John, wagon-maker, res s s Stuart, 6th e of Twelfth
Fastre, Wm, laborer, bds at Waterloo House
Fay, Frank, upholster, 98 Washington, bds w s Adams, 3d s of Main
Fealder, Ludolf, wagon-maker, res ne cor Crooks and Clay
Featherly, J S, res 139 Walnut
Febrey, Mrs Susan, seamstress, bds 250 Adams
Fedler, J C, broker, res s s Walnut, 5th e of Clay
Felschner, C, butcher, 168 Washington
Felthousen, J, carpenter, res 65 Twelfth
Ferron, A, laborer, bds Waterloo House
Ferris, Miss Mary E, principal East River School
Field, W Jr, insurance ag't office, 111 Washington, res De-Pere
Finan, Mike, mason, res s s Cass, 1st e of Adams
Findeisen, L, tinsmith, bds w s Washington, 2d s of Crooks
Finnegan, Annie, 226 Jefferson
Finnegan, Mrs Jane, wid, res ne cor Pine and Adams
Finnegan, Mary ne cor Quincy and Cass
Finnegan, Mary, ne cor Monroe and Chicago
Finnegan, Mike, drayman, res 13 Quincy
First, Fred, sawyer, res s s Doty, 1st e of Twelfth
First National Bank
First Presbyterian Church, w s Adams, 2d s of Crooks

FISK WM J, Vice Pres't Kellogg National Bank, res Ft Howard

Fritzharris, Kate, sw cor Walnut and Webster

Flaherty, Patrick, laborer, 270 Walnut

Flatley, D, liveryman, s s Pine 2d e Adams, res 188 Main

Flatley, J, dry goods, 79 Washington, res sw cor Pine and Quincy

Flatley, Mike, clerk, 79 Washington, bds se cor Pine and Quincy

Flath, W, harness-maker, e s Washington nr Walnut, res n s Walnut, 2d e of Jackson

Flayley, Sarah, e s Monroe, 2d s of Lawe

Fleming, John, drayman, res s s Cedar, 1st e of Monroe

Flhaw, Martin, laborer, res 2d story, No 34 Main

Flintville Stage Line Office, City Hotel

Florence, Chas, laborer, res s s Cedar, 1st e of Clay

Flump, Simon, harness-maker, res n s Cherry, 2d w of Twelfth

Fohrmann, Ioseph, Sr, merchant, 102 Washington, res 255 Adams

Fohrmann, Jos Jr, clerk 102 Washington, res 255 Adams

Fohrmann, Lizzie, Green Bay House

Follett, B, books and stationary, 124 Washington, res e s Jefferson, 2d s of Walnut

Follett, D F, printer, Gazette office, bds Adams House

Follett, D I, editor Gazette, res w s Adams 2d s of Walnut

Follett, E W, res e s Adams, 2d s of Walnut

Follett, Geo, tinner, res s s Walnut, 3d e of Clay

Follett, Henry, printer, res e s Jefferson, 2d s of Stuart

Follett, J W, books, 124 Washington, res e s Adams, 2d s of Walnut

Follett, W, tinsmith, n s Cherry, 2d e of Washington, res 181 Washington

Fontain, Benj, hardware, store and res s s Main, 4th w of Adams

Fontain, Paul, blacksmith, res s s Mason, 2d w of Goodell

FORTIER, C L, physician, 94 Washington, res w s Jackson 3d s of Stuart

Forsyth, Catharine, cook at Minnesota House

Foster, Christian, tailor, res n s Crooks, 3d w of Eleventh

Foster, Louis, painter, res ne cor Walnut and Clay

Fox, Paul, merchant, 142 Washington st, res sw cor Cherry and Monroe

Fox, Peter, merchant, 142 Washington, res sw cor Cherry and Monroe

Fox River House, cor of Washington and Cherry

Francart, Francois, laborer, res ns Cass, 1st w of Twelfth
Franck, Chas, teamster, res 302 Washington
Franck, M, clerk, VanNostrand, Klause & Co, res 302 Washington
Franck, P, street commissioner, res 302 Washington
Francee, Francis, res s s Elm, 1st w of city limits
Frank, S, pedlar, res 202 Cherry
Franklin Fire Co No 3, sw cor Main and Twelfth
Franks, Mary, se cor Jefferson and Walnut
Fransens, John, harness-maker, res w s Jackson, 2d n Chicago
Fransil, Josephene, n w cor Cherry and Jackson
Fray, Elmer, rag dealer, res n s Elm, city limits
Frantz, Mary, 283 Adams
Freadel, John, carpenter, res s s Cherry, 4th e of Clay
FREEMAN, H G, cashier Kellogg Nat Bank, bds 266 Adams
French Catholic Church, Milwaukee, bet Jefferson & Madison
French, G B, express messenger, C N W R R
French Presbyterian Church, n s Doty bet Adams and Jefferson
Frewert, Peter, mason, res 108 Cedar
Friend, Chas D, turner, res 357 Cherry
Friend, F A, turner, res 357 Cherry
Friend, Geo D, laborer, res No 357 Cherry
Frisque, Florentine, tailor, shop and res e s Jackson, 1st s of Walnut
Fruipont, Prospere, res 285 Stuart
Fulkerson, Hiram, express teamster, bds 265 Adams
Fuller, Chas, real estate dealer, bds at Beaumont House

G

Gaffney, Mike, lumberman, bds at Minnesota House
Gagnon, Maxime, barber, 135 Washington, res 220 Madison
Gaines, D C, clerk, American Express office, Shaylor's blk, cor Adams and Pine
Galager, Jas, well-digger, bds n s Main, 3d w of Twelfth
Galaher, Lizzie, s s Howard, 1st e of Jefferson
Ganthier, J B, laborer, res sw cor Chicago and Baird
Ganycan, Alex, laborer, ne cor Eleventh and Cedar
Ganycan, Frank, res se cor Eleventh and Cedar
Gapp, Claude, laborer, res n s Main, 4th e of Webster
Garbsch, H, proprietor of bakery, s s Main, bet Washington and Adams
Gardapie, Louisa, chambermaid, Beaumont House
Gardner, B, machinist, res e s Monroe, 2d s of Chicago

Garl, Andrew, laborer, res n s Stuart, 2d w of Eleventh
GARNER, W M, restaurant, res No 35 Pine
Garot, Frank, laborer, res No 40 Madison st
Garrigan, Mrs Lizzie, bds Tremont House
Gass, Louis, confectioner, 249 Walnut
Gassling, Veronica, 139 Monroe
Gassogne, E, stone-cutter, res n s Elm, 3d e of St George
Gaylord, G A, lake captain, res se cor Quincy and Mason
Gebean, Chas, mason, res 216 Madison
Gehy, Fred, barkeeper, e s of Washington, 2d s of Main
Gehacks, Annie, n s Crooks, bet Webster and Clay
Genett, Julia, w s Jefferson, 1st s of Mason
Genine, Louis, marble-cutter, Green Bay marble works
German Luthern Church, ne cor Cherry and VanBuren st
Gertang, W, laborer, res Astor saloon building
Geyer, D, proprietor of saloon, 121 Washington, res w s St
    George, 1st n of Elm
Gesland, A, yardman, Beaumont House
Geyske, John, teamster, res s s Chicago, 1st w of East
    River
Gher, Peter, miller, bds sw cor Quincy and Cedar
Gibson, Rev, res sw cor Walnut and Jefferson
Gibson, Jas, res n s Pine, 3d w of Quincy
Giese, Aug, carpenter, res e s Quincy, 3d s of Grignon
Giese, M, gardner, res e s Quincy, 3d s of Grignon
Gieseler, Herman, book-keeper, 60 Washington, res w s of
    Quincy, 1st n of Stuart
Gieseler, Otto, traveling ag't, bds w s Quincy, 1st n of Stuart
Giesgler, Ed, deputy sheriff, res 279 Adams
Gilbert, W H B, river captain, res SS Pine st
Gilden, John, hackman, bds e s Jefferson, 2d s of Cherry
Gilligan, John, tinner, res s s Pine, 1st w of VanBuren
GLAHN, FRED, cigar dealer, 44 Pine, res e s Quincy, 2d n of
    Doty
Glaser, Geo, laborer, res e s St George, 4th n of Elm
Glass, Fred, carpenter and joiner, bds at Minnesota House
Glass, J J, teamster, bds n s Walnut, 2d e of Eleventh
Gleison, Bridget, se cos Madison & Crooks
Globe Printing Office, 122 Washington
Godfrey, Jos, cooper, res 78 Elm
Godfrey, Levi B, contractor, res 323 Adams
Godfrey, O S, book-keeper, Green Bay Iron Works, res 323
    Adams
Goebel, John, proprietor of Farmers House, nw cor Cedar
    and Twelfth

ROBINSON & BRO.,

Green Bay Advocate,

ESTABLISHED IN 1846.

JOB PRINTERS,

AND BOOK BINDERS!!

36 PINE STREET.

GREEN BAY, WISCONSIN.

Goetzman, Miss Barbara, res nw cor Main and Twelfth
Goffort, Albert, carpenter, res s s Elm, 2d e of St George
Goldammer, Rev C F, res n s Cherry, 2d e of VanBuren
Goldammer, Chas, merchant, res n s Cherry, 2d e of Van-Buren
Goldammer, Theo, wagon-maker, res n s Cherry, 2d e of VanBuren
Golden, Ellen, 234 Jefferson
Goodell, Nathan, book-keeper, res Adams, 3d s of Walnut
Goodfellow, Robert, book-keeper, at elevator, res 45 Stuart
Goodhue, Miss F D, res w s Jackson, 2d n of Lawe
Goodhue, Miss N M, res w s Jackson, 2d n of Lawe
Goodhing, J F, accountant, Green Bay & M R R Offices
Goodnough, Arthur, clerk, 146 Washington
Gorden, Miss Ida, assistant principal at high school
Goodya, Mary, seamstress, nw cor Webster and Doty
Goron, Sam'l, shoemaker, res 216 Madison
GOTTO, ELI, clerk, s s Main, 3d w of Adams
Gotto, Miss Flora, clerk, dry-goods, under Beaumont House
Gotto, J, dry-goods and clothing, under Beaumont House, res n s Pine, 2d e of Quincy
Gould, Albert, carpenter, bds n s Walnut, 1st w of Twelfth
Gould, Chas, steamboat engineer, res 381 Walnut st
Gould, Edwin, sup't Green Bay Hide and Leather Co, res 318 Main
Grady, Jas, plasterer, res s s Cass, 2d e of Adams
Graff, Jos, carpenter, res w s Eleventh, 1st n of Walnut
Graves, Jos, carpenter, res s s main, 3d e of Webster
Graner, Rob't, cattle-dealer, res n s Main, 3d e of Webster
Grant, Peter, harness-maker, res n s of Madison, 3d n of Cass
Graves, A W, painter, bds Fox River House
Grave, Frank, planer, res 341 Walnut
Graves, Frank, laborer, bds United States Hotel
Grave, J P, carpenter, res 341 Walnut
Grave, J, laborer, bds United States Hotel
Graves, O B, attorney, 120 Washington, res town of Prebel
Grebling, M, tinner, 155 and 157 Washington
Greely, M F, cutter, 105 Washington, res s s Walnut, 3d e of Quincy
Green, A, carpenter, res n s Stuart, 2d e of Eleventh
Green, Carrie, nw cor Madison and Lawe
Green, Gustave, laborer, res ne cor Stuart and Eleventh
GREEN, G G, attorney, cor pine and Adams, bds 132 Main
Green, Jacob, laborer, res ne cor Stuart and Eleventh
Green, Dr J, office and res No 1 Spring st

Green, P R, commission Merchant, e s of Washington, 5th s ol Walnut, res ne cor Doty and Jefferson
Green Bay Advocate, 36 Pine st
Green Bay Business College, 3d floor, 151 and 153 Washington st
Green Bay Gas Works, n s Elm, bet Madison and Jefferson
Green Bay House, cor Main and Adams
Green Bay Iron Co
Green Bay Laundry, w s Washington, 3d s of Crooks
Green Bay Lodge I O O F, 2d s 51 Cherry
Green Bay Marble Works, s s Cherry, 1st e of Adams
Green Bay & M R R Depot, Ft Howard, crossing of N W Railroad
Green Bay & M R R Office, cor Pine and Adams
Green Bay VolksZeitung, 38 Pine, 2d floor
Gref, John, butcher, 158 Washington, bds the same
Grignon, D H, attorney and police justice, 153 Washington, res point of Jefferson and Portage
Grogan Peter, blacksmith, bds at Minnesota House
Grimm, Jos, res nw cor Quincy and Eliza
Grasle, Geo, brewer in East River brewery, w s Twelfth, 1st s of Cedar
Grossen, John, res ne cor Main and Clay
Grossen, Louis, res ne cor Main and Clay
Grossen, Stephen, saloon and res ne cor Main and Clay
Grosswinkel, Peter, laborer, res 210 VanBuren
Grothe, Jacob, brewer, in East River brewery
Grunert, B G, editor Green Bay VolksZeitung, res sw cor Walnut and Jackson
Guddfried, Leidel, miller, res 91 Twelfth st
GUESNIER, ALEX SR, attorney and real estate, 95 Washington, res nw cor Cherry and Clay
Guesnier, Alex Jr, book-keeper, res nw cor Cherry and Clay
Guesnier, clerk, res nw cor Cherry and Clay
Guesnier, Jos, student
Guimont, D, barkeeper, 97 Washington
Gunn, Edward, painter, res n s Cherry, 3d w of Quincy
Gunn, Hugh, mason, res n s Cherry, 3d w of Quincy
Gunn, Jas, mason, res n s Cherry, 3d w of Quincy
Gusee, Fred, shoemaker, bds at United States Hotel

H

Haff, Rev F R, rector St James Episcopal Church, res w s Quincy 2d n of Crooks
Hagensen, Mary, servant, 300 Adams

HAGEMEISTER, FRANK, meat-market, e s Adams, 1st n
Pine, res ne cor Pine and Adams
HAGENMEISTER, H, butcher, res cor Pine and Adams
Hagen, F A, livery stable, w s Adams bet Pine and Cherry,
res s s Cherry, 2d e Monroe
Hagerty, John, livery stable, cor Walnut and Washington, res
44 Walnut
Hagen, H, clerk, bds Adams House
Hagen, P, laborer, bds U S Hotel
Hagen, Emil, laborer, bds St Louis House
Hagerty, John Jr, res 44 Walnut
Hair, Lena, servant, Bay City House
Hall, Minnie, servant, w s Monroe, 3d n Chicago
Hall, P, servant, e s Monroe, 1st n of Crooks
HALL, E L, jeweler, 95 Washington, res n s Pine, 2d e of
Madison
Hall, Edward W, photographer, 85 Washington, res s s Pine,
3d n of Clay
Hall, C H, carpenter, res n s Cherry, 7th e of Twelfrh
Hall, Chas A, carpenter, res s s Cherry, 6th e of Twelfth
Hall, H E, express messenger, C N W R R bds restaurant
Hall, Horace, gunsmith, 96 Washington, res w s Jefferson, 2d
s Walnut
Haltman, Annie, servant, 109 Madison
Haly, William Rev, pastor M E Church, (German,) res nw
cor Doty and Clay
Hambitzen, Joseph, tinner, 113 Washington, res sw cor Cher-
ry and Jackson
Hambitzen, William, res sw cor Cherry and Jackson
Hamilton, Andrew, furnaceman, bds 239 Main
Hamilton, Wm, stationery engineer, res 251 Main
Hamilton, Miss Sarah D, teacher in Pine st school
Hamlin, Fred, mason, res sw cor Crooks and VanBuren
Hamlin, Henry, carpenter, res 121 Monroe
Hamm, John, shoemaker, res 361 Adams
Hamm, Louis, laborer, res 315 Jefferson
Hamm, P, teamster, American Express Co, res Shaylor blk
Hamm, Mary, servant, s s Law 1st e of Jefferson
Hanan, Frank, res w s Jefferson, 3d n Cass
Hancock, W R, treasurer, G B & M R R, office Shaylor blk,
res — Walnut
Hansen, Sophy, servant, 139 Madison
Harson, Gunder, laborer, res 70 Eleventh st
Hanson, Nettie, servant, e s VanBuren, 1st n Chicago
Hanson, Annie, servant, 411 Lawe
Hanson, Sam'l, 2d porter Beaumont House

Hanz, Fred, laborer, res s s Walnut, 2d w of Eleventh
Hart, Asahel, pile-driver, bds 129 Monre
Harbridge, Jas, foreman, Bertam's stave manufactory, res s s
    Cherry, 3d w Monroe
Harder, O L, saw repairer, 39 Pine, res 137 Monroe
Harder, Francis, gunsmith, res 149 Cherry
Harmon, Frank, carpenter, res n s Doty, 2d w of Eleventh
Harnos, L, butcher, res s s Cherry, 5th e of Fox River House
Harran, D, horse-dealer, res nw cor Cherry and Quincy
Harrigan, Mrs R O,
Harriman, L H, liveryman, e s of Jefferson, 2d and 3d s Cherry
Harris, ——, laborer, res s s Pine, 2d e of VanBuren
Harris, S C, furnaceman, bds 239 Mason
Harris, T E, hardware merchant, 38 Pine, res 131 Monroe
Harris, E P, foreman at G B Iron Works, bds 239 Mason
HARTEAU, D M, architect, No 4 Shaylor's blk, res ne cor
    Cedar and Webster
Hartung, Chas, hardware merchant, 160 Washington, res w s
    Quincy, 2d s Doty
HARTEAU, S W, dry-goods, 118 Washington, res s s Howard
    2d w of Madison
Hartman, Joseph, painter, bds St Louis House
Hartshorn, D G, express messenger, C & N W R R, bds
    First National Hotel
Hasseil, Anton, mason, n s Doty, 1st e of Clay
HASTINGS, S D JR, attorney, office cor Pine and Adams, res
    e s Monroe, 2d s Lawe
Hatch, S H, engineer and machinist, res e s Jackson, 2d n of
    Mason
Hatch, Dell G, teamster, res w s Jackson, 1st s Mason
Hawks, A D, clerk, res 20 St Clair
Hawks, Miss Fannie, clerk, 91 Washington, bds 203 Adams
Hays, Mary, servant, 225 Jefferson
Hays, Frank, printer Herald office, bds e s Washington, 4th s
    Stuart
Heiser, Mena, servant, 409 Lawe
Heinkleman, Wm, bar-keeper, 121 Washington, res w s
    Quincy, 1st n Grignon
Heinkleman, Christian, laborer, res w s Eleventh, 2d n Cass
Heinkleman, Otto, mason, res w s Eleventh, 2d n Cass
Heirch, E G, law student, 120 Washington, bds Whitney
    House Ft Howard
Heller, William, laborer, s s Cherry, 4th e of Twelfth
Hendricks, John, ominbns ticket ag't on R R, res s s Cherry,
    1st n Eleventh, or bds at Beaumont House
Henkelmunn, Fred, laborer, w s Adams, 4th s Cass

Hendricks, John, saloon, 277 Main, res the same
Hendricks, C W, dry goods and groceries, 47 Main, res the same
Hendricks, Jane Mrs, wid, bds 47 Main
Hendricks, Desire, laborer, 345 Crooks
Henricks, Anton, laborer, res s s Walnut, 2d e Quincy
Hentz, Aug, laborer, Gas Works, res Ft Howard
Henry, Jacob, laborer, n s Elm, 2d w Monroe
Henshall, Rev J G, minister in charge of Baptist Church, cor Madison and Moravian
Herbegneux, J B, laborer, bds w s Adams, 4th n of Pine
Hermann, John, book-binder, 124 Washington, res No 41 Twelfth
Herman, Anton, shoemaker, 112 Washington
Herring, Joseph, furnaceman, res s s Cedar, 3d n VanBuren
HERSCHEDE, E MRS, Queen City Restaurent, 38 Pine
Heyd, Conrad, artist, sw cor Pine and Cherry
Heyrman, Joseph, city engineer, res 254 Crooks
Hickey, Mary, head waitress, Beaumont House
Hickox, Susan B Mrs, wid, res 121 Monroe
Hienrits, Henry, wagon-maker, Main nr East River bridge, res n s Cedar, 2d w Twelfth
High School, n s School, bet Monroe and Madison
Hildebran, Peter, laborer, n s Doty, 4th e Clay
Hildebran, Mary, servant, e s Quincy, 1st s Mason
Hill, Royal, general contractor, res se cor Eleventh and St Clair
Hills, J P, harness-shop, 147 Washington, res s s Pine, 3d w Jefferson
Hils, Christian
Hills, Peter, laborer, res 300 Cedar
Hinks, Thomas, res n s Cherry, 2d e Clay
Hinsk, Mary, servant, n s Pine, 1st e Adams
Hinsdale, U C, express messenger, G B & M R R, bds 108 Walnut
Hoeffel, Louis, proprietor Astor Mills, cor Washington and Doty, res 242 Jefferson
Hoeffel, Julius, clerk with Philip Klaus, bds 242 Jefferson
Hoeffel, S, miller, res 244 Jefferson
Hoes, E V B. teller First National Bank
Hoffen, Rev Father, pastor in charge of Holland Catholic Church
Hoelter. Frederick, bakery, n s Main, 2d e Clay, res the same
Hoekle, Rev Wm, minister in charge of German Methodist Society

Hoffman, M J, painter, res w s Jackson, 1st n Doty
HOFFMAN, WM merchant tailor, 105 Washington, res se cor Chicago and VanBuren
Hoffman, August, laborer, ne cor Stuart and Clay
Hoffman, Henry, hostler, n s Adams bet Pine and Cherry
Hoffmeister, H, blacksmith, e s Washington, 2d n Crooks
Hoffmeister, Emma, servant, nw cor Pine and Jackson
Hoffman, Geo, blacksmith, bds Whittington House
Hogan, Bridget, servant, 168 Main
Hole, Hennan, tailor, res n s Doty, 2d e Clay
Holland Catholic Church, cor Adams and Doty
Hollman, Fred, commercial traveller, res 271 Adams
HOLLMAN, HENRY, dry goods, 103 Washington, bds 271 Adams
HOLMES, A G E, dry goods, 118 Washington, res 168 Jefferson
Holmes, B M, saw-mill, n s Pine, 3d e Madison
Holsknecht, Matthias, boots and shoes, s s Main, 2d w Jefferson, res ne cor Jackson and Stuart
Holton, Nora, servant, 234 Jefferson
Holtz, Minnie Mrs, wid, nw cor Webster and Pine
Holzer, Barbara, servant, 200 Jefferson
Hopkins, Frank, express messenger, G B & M R R, bds 108 Walnut
Hood, A, laborer, res 335 Cedar
Hoppe, Otto, tailor, res s s Cherry, 3d w Twelfth
Hoppe, Albert, tailor, w s Walnut, 3d w Twelfth, res the same
Hord, Lewis, servant, ne cor Cherry and Monroe
Horlbut, Frederick, res sw cor Cherry and Madison
Horn, Katie, servant, ne cor Cherry and Quincy
Horner, Chas, currier, res s s Main, 2d e river
Horrigan, Annie Miss, compositor Advocate office, res Ft Howard
Hory, John, tailor, res 234 Cherry
Hoskinson, Geo, proprietor State Gazette, res w s Madison, 4th s Stuart
Hounter, Annie, servant, 101 Cherry
House, J, lumberman, bds Fox River House
Howe, T O, attorney, res 173 Main
Howell, Jane Mrs, wid, res e s Eleventh, 1st n Main
Howell, Roland, carpenter, res e s Eleventh, 1st n Main
Hoye, Mary, servant, s s Cherry, 2d n Quincy
Hrabik, Jos, tailor, 105 Washington, res s s Walnut, 2d e Quincy
Huber, Martin billard-rooms, e s Washington, 2d s Main, res 147 Quincy

HUDD, T R, attorney, office cor Washington and Pine, res cor Jefferson and Cherry
Huhl, Peter, servant, 118 Main
Huinger, G, groceries, and hardware, n s Main, 4th e Quincy res 197 Main
Huinger, T W, apprentice, Geo Merkle, res 197 Main
Hume, Wm Mrs, matron Cadle Home
Hummel, A, res se cor Jefferson and Willow
Hun, Leonard, tanner, s s Main, 1st w Twelfth
Hunter, Alvin, proprietor G B & Flintville, stage line, office City Hotel
HUNTINGTON, H J, attorney, office Chapman's blk, res s s Crooks, 3d e Jackson
Hupper, H Rev,
Hutseck, John, tanner, res n s Main, 3d w Clay
Hylitchker, Mary, servant, 301 Monroe

I

Ichey, Emma, w s Monroe, 2d n of Chicago
Ingalls, G H, photographer, 85 Washington, bds 222 Main
Ingalls, J, lumber dealer, res 222 Main
Ingersoll, E B, res n s Walnut, 2d w Webster
Irr, Miss Caroline M, res ne cor Stuart and Twelfth
Irr, Miss Clara, res ne cor Stuart and Twelfth
Irr, Oliver, res ne cor Stuart and Twelfth
Irwin, Mrs A J, wid, res 105 Main

J

Jacobs, Hans, laborer, res n s Cherry, 4th w of Twelfth
Jacobs, J B, supervisor, 2d ward, res 411 Lawe
Jacobs, J B Jr, book-keeper, Taylor & Duncan, res 411 Lawe
Jacobs, Alex, deliverer, W B Carpenter, res 411 Lawe
Jacobi, Arthur, civil engineer, s s Cherry 2d w Eleventh
Jacobi, Arthur M, clerk, ne cor Pine and Washington, res s s Cherry, 2d w Eleventh
Jackson Square, bet Madison and Monroe s of Doty
Jansen, Mary, laundress, Steam Laundry, bds nw cor Quincy and Chicago
Jansen, Chas, tinner, res s s Cherry, 2d w Twelfth
Jaujauer, Joseph, clerk, City Hotel, cor Washington and Walnut
Jax, Peter, carpenter, res 330 Stuart
Jeffcott, Sarah Mrs, wid, res 171 Walnut
Jeffcott, Chas, clerk, 49 Pine, res 171 Walnut
Jeffrey, J S Mrs, wid, res ne cor Jefferson and Walnut

Jeffrey, F, butcher, 158 Washington, bds same
Jenins, Frank, laborer, res w s Eleventh, 2d s Cedar
Jennewein, John, book-binder, Advocate office, bds Whittington House
Jenny, A D, ticket agent, C & N W R R, bds Beaumont House
Jensen, Neil, bds 239 Main
Jensen, Jennie Mrs, boarding house, e s Washington, 4th s Stuart
Jeziur, August, laborer, res s s Lawe, 1st w Baird
Jinesy, A, foundryman, res se cor Cherry and Clay
JOANNES, CHAS, grocer, 120 Washington, res e s Quincy
JOANNES, FELIX, grocer, 120 Washington, res 126 Quincy
JOANNES, DAN, grocer, 120 Washington, res n s Crooks, 1st e Monroe
JOANNES, W M, grocer, 120 Washington, res 126 Quincy
JOANNES, MITCHELL, grocer, 120 Washington, res 126 Quincy
JOANNES, THOMAS, grocer, 120 Washington, res 126 Quincy
Jobelius, John, saloon keeper, ne cor Main and Twelfth res same
Joblius, Jacob, carpenter, res 338 Crooks
Johns, Minnie, waitress Beaumont House
Johnson, Martin, bridge-tender, e s Monroe, 1st s Porlier
Johnson, Bertha, kitchen girl, Beaumont House
Johnson, John W, carpenter, bds e s Monroe, 1st s Porlier
Johnson, M, engineer furnace, res in rear of furnace
Johnson, Sarah, servant, e s Monroe, 1st n Crooks
Johnson, Collett, servant, 176 Madison
Johnson, Emma, servant, 69 Cherry
Johnson, Maria, servant, 141 Walnut
Johnson, Bertha, servant, 23 Milwaukee
Johnson, Chas, tanner, s s Main, 2d w Twelfth
Johnson, Peter, carpenter, res 247 Main
John, Frederick, saloon, 104 Washington st, res s s Cherry, 1st e Eleventh
John, Geo, foundryman, res w s Eleventh, 2d s Cedar
Jolie, Louis, laborer, res se cor Chicago and Twelfth
Jolie, Joseph, laborer, res se cor Chicago and Twelfth
JONES, PORTER, printer, res e s Madison. 3d n Doty
Jones, Martin, attorney, res s s Doty, 9th e Twelfth
Jones, Bridget Mrs, wid, res n s Main, 3d e Twelfth
Jones, S B, mason, bds n s Main, 3d w Twelfth
Jones, Thomas, laborer, res 360 Cedar
Jorden, Christian, laborer, n s Stuart, 3d e Twelfth
Jordain, T L, printer Advocate office, bds Whittington House

Jorgensen, John L, clerk, 91 Washington, res 221 Adams
Juch, Chas, cigar manufactory, s s Walnut, 1st w Washington, res the same
Juen, Adaline Mrs, wid, res n s Stuart, 2d w Webster
JUEUGER J P, saloon keeper, 141 Washington, res cor monroe and Stuart
July, Jacob, tailor, res s s Walnut, 1st w Adams
Juneau, E, proprietor City Hotel, cor Washington and Walnut st
Juneau, Mrs, wid, res w s Washington, 2d s Crooks
Junk, John, hostler, Three Corner House
Justins, Joseph, carpenter, res w s Quincy, 2d n Main

K

Kalb, Jas, meat-market, 158 Washington, also on Main, res 158 and 160 Washington
Kampton, A, laborer, res s s Main, 1st w Webster
Kane, Kate Miss, w s VanBuren, 1st n Doty
Kane, Ella Mrs, wid, res w s VanBuren, 1st n Doty
Kane, John, carpenter, bds Minnesota House
Kanny, Chas, porter Adams House
Kaster, C, tailor, 37 Pine, res s s Cherry, 2d e Clay
Kaufmann, F, clerk, Bay City House
Keel, Fred, bus-driver, Hagans Livery, bds restaurant
Keetches, Frank, saddler, res n s Stuart, 1st w Eleventh
Keeth, J E, law-student, with Hastings and Green, bds 176 Madison
Kellogg, C W, sash, doors and blinds etc, n s Cedar 2d w of Adams, res e s Jefferson, 3d n of Crooks
Kehler, John, carpenter, res 337 Jefferson
KELLOGG NATIONAL BANK, 132 Washington
KELLOGG, R B, president Kellogg National Bank, bds 254 Washington
Keller, Mary, cook, City Hotel
KELLY, D M, vice president and general manager, G B & M R R, office Shaylor blk, bds Beaumont House
Kemp, Amanda, res 259 Walnut
Kemp, Wm, house numberer, res 259 Walnut
Kemp, Chas, helmsman steamer, res 259 Walnut
Kendall, P R, commission merchant, 140 Washington, res w s Jackson, 2d n Lawe
Kendall, E L, commission merchant, 140 Washington, res w s Madison, 1st s Cedar
Kennedy, F, piano dealer, bds Beaumont House
KENRICK, S B, suprintendant G B & M R R, bds se cor Monroe and Doty

Kensler, Frank, saloon keeper, n s Walnut, 1st w Washington, res se cor Quincy and Crooks
Kensler, Geo, res se cor Quincy and Crooks
Kenyon, G W, wagon-maker, e s Adams, 2d s Main, res — Main
Kern, Henry, carpenter, res n s Stuart, 3d e Eleventh
Kernin, Edward J, foreman, Burkhart's furniture manufactory, res e s VanBuren 2d s Stuart
Kerr, Jas, printer Gazette Office, bds Ft Howard
Kersten, Theodore, carpenter, 316 Stuart
Kersten, Geo, carpenter, 316 Stuart
Ketter, Michael, laborer, res e s Webster, 2d s Doty
Kersten, Eva Miss, compositor, Volks Zietung office, res 316 Stuart
Kersten, Anton, apprentice, Volks Zietung office, res 316 Stuart
Keyser, Gerardus D, laborer, res s s Crooks, 2d e Clay
Keyes, Geo M, salesman, 32 and 34 Pine
Keyes, Edward C, salesman, 32 and 34 Pine
Kienth, John, druggist, 49 Main, res s s Main, 3d e of Jefferson
Kies, C H, justice of peace, 2d floor, 153 Washington, res w s Webster, 2d n Crooks
Killian, J A, city marshal, res w s Monroe, 2d s Washington
Kiley, Kate, servant, 252 Washington
Kimball, Alonzo, hardware, 155 and 157 Washington, res e s Adams, 2d s Stuart
Kimball, Mather D, printer and binder, office 122 Washington, res e s Adams, 2d s Stuart
Kimball, C T, clerk, res w s Jefferson, 3d n Chicago
KIMBALL, A W, insurance agency, office 122 Washington, res 252 Washington
King, Benj, res 71 Cedar
King, D W, druggist, cor Washington and Walnut, res sw cor Jefferson and Walnut
King, Chas, brewer, bds St Louis House
King, E W, Jr, clerk, D W King, res nw cor Jefferson and Walnut
Kintop, John, clerk, at 142 Washington
Kippenberry, Katie, servant, w s Quincy, 3d s Chicago
Kirk, William, clerk, bds se cor Pine and VanBuren
Kitchen, Chas, city bakery, 139 Washington, res — Cherry
Kittner, Annie, servant, 188 Mason
KITTNER, EDWARD, carriage maker, cor Washington and Doty, res e s Washington, 2d s Stuart
Kittner, Emil, student, res e s Washington, 3d s Stuart

Kittner, John, res e s Washington, 3d s Stuart
Klaus, Chas, res n s Pine, 2d w Jackson
Klaus, P, fancy goods, res sw cor Pine and Monroe
Klaus, Appolma, servant, s s Pine, 2d e Quincy
Klaus, Alonis, life insurance, res 328 Main
Klaus, Joseph, butcher, 205 Main, res w s Clay, 2d n Main
Klaus, Anton, lumber, also wholesale dry goods and groceries, res se cor Jefferson and Crooks
Klaus, Hall, No 40, 42 and 44 Pine
Klausen, T, carpenter, res w s Washington, 3d s Crooks
Klemak, Valanty, foundryman, s s Stuart, 2d e Twelfth
Klemak, Andry, foundryman, s s Stuart, 2d e Twelfth
Klemak, Nichol, foundryman, s s Stuart, 2d e Twelfth
Klingenberg, R, liquor dealer, 42 Pine, res 263 Adams
Kobalski, Frank, shoemaker, s s Stuart, 1st w Twelfth
KOCH, O, wholesale grocer, 92 Washington, res Ft Howard
Koenig, Gustoff, laborer, res n s Stuart, 5th e Twelfth
Konowski, Peter, laborer, res s s Crooks, 2d w Baird
Kontop, Thomas, laborer, s s Stuart, 1st e Twelfth
Kooherr, Frank, tinner 87 Washington st
Kopper, John, East River Brewery, bds the same
Korl, Joseph, laborer, res 363 Stuart
Kowalski, Augusta, e s Jefferson, 2d s Pine
Kox, Anton, laborer, res n s Crooks, 1st w Baird
Koye, Joseph, mason, res nw cor Twelfth and Elm
Krop, Frank, mail-carrier, Green Bay to Two Rivers, res s s Cedar, 1st w Twelfth
Krause, Peter, mason, res 296 Walnut
Kramer, Mat, clerk, Green Bay House, cor Main and Adams
Kreosky, John, brick maker, s s Chicago, 2d w E River
Krisel Kate, w s Quincy, 2d s Stuart
Kroeger, Lousa, dining-room girl, Bay City House
Kross, Fred, first porter Beaumout House
Kulzberg, Anton, tanner, res n s Doty, 2d w Twelfth
Kucher, Chas O, machinist, bds City Hotel
Kuhlman, Gustave, salesman, 32 and 34 Pine, bds Whittington House
Kukrl, Frank, blacksmith, res s s Doty, 2d e Clay
Kurtz, G D, tinner, res nw cor Webster and Pine
Kurtz, Gotleib, marble cutter, at G B marble works
Kurshka, Martin, E River Brewery, res 47 Twelfth
Kustermann, G, music-dealer, 122 Washington, res w s Monroe, 1st s Cherry
Kustermann, Carl, clerk, 125 Washington, res nw cor Jackson and Crooks

16

Kustermann, Rob't, clerk, G Sommers, bds nw cor Crooks and Jackson

Kyber, G E T, insurance, collecting and passenger agent, 2d floor, 102 Washington, res Allonez

L

LaBart, S, grocer, n s Main, 3d e Adams

Labore, Albert, res n s Chicago, 1st e Monroe

Lacourt, Anton, shoemaker, s s Walnut, 2d e Jackson

Lacourt, Prosper, shoemaker, n s Cherry, 3d e Clay

Lake, Martin, res s s Crooks, 3d w VanBuren

Laflower, Joseph, cooper, bds 222 Main

LAMARRÉ, CONSTANCE, flour and feed, 78 Washington, res e s Adams, 2d s River

LAMB, G A, physician, office 2d story, 160 Washington, res s e cor Jefferson and Walnut

Lamb, Willard, lumber merchant, res nw cor Crooks and Webster

Lamb, C Miss, student, bds 2d story 45 Cherry

Lambdin, H S, telegraph operator, W C R R depot, bds 267 Adams

LAMPSON, F M, painter, res s s Walnut, 4th w Adams

Lander, M J, attorney, office 2d story 148 Washington

Lange, H, carriage trimmer for A Weise, res n s Walnut, 2d e of Monroe

Landwehr, S, proprietor Green Bay House, cor Adams and Main

LANGLOIS, J B, proprietor Home saloon, 115 Washington, res 100 Cherry

Langlois, F H, clerk, J B Langlois, bds 100 Cherry

Langton, Jemima Mrs, wid, res 133 Jefferson

LANGTON, G N, feed store, 106 Washington, res 133 Jefferson

Langton, C T, drives express wagon, res 133 Jefferson

Langton, Geo, bds 133 Jefferson

Lantz, Otto, clerk, 103 Washington, bds Whittington House

Lapine, Louis, ship carpenter, res n s Stuart, 5th e Clay

Laporte, Eugene, 17 School

Larsen, Mary, w s Webster, 1st n Crooks

Larsen, Julia, e s Webster, 1st n Crooks

Larose, Sophy Miss, res w s Jackson, 2d s Monroe

Larsheid, Lawrence, carpenter, res n s of Walnut, 1st s of Twelfth

Larsheid, M, teamster, res nw cor Stuart and Twelfth

Lassig, Edward, sawyer, res nw cor Webster and Doty

Last, John B, res 49 Stuart

Latham, M, manager, Northwestern Telegraph, 107 Washington, bds 1st National Hotel

Lank, Mary, Adams House, w s Adams, 1st n Cherry

Lantz. Aug, book-keeper, 1st National Bank

, Lawe, John D, grocer, 49 Pine, res 211 Adams

Lawrence, John, laborer, res 293 Madison

Lawrence, Edward, boiler maker, res n s Stuart, 2d w of Twelfth

LAWRENCE, P, liquor dealer, 136 Washington, res e s Washington, 5th s Stuart

Lawrence, Chas, hostler at Hagen's livery stable, bds Adams House

Lawrence Park on E River, bet Crooks and Chicago

LAWTON, G A, president National Bank of Commerce, cor Washington and Pine, res 23 Milwaukee

Leanna, Comb, carpenter, res w s Quincy, 2d n Chicago

Leanna, Lepolian, car tender, res w s Quincy, 2d n Chicago

Lebert, James, laborer, w s Webster, 1st n Crooks

Lebert, James, laborer, res 228 VanBuren

Lecop, Frank, umbrella maker, res w s Jefferson, 2d e of Elm

LeClair, Chas, res 243 Monroe

LeClair, Chas A, sailor, res 243 Monroe

LeClair, Joseph, sailor, res 243 Monroe

LeClaire, Joseph B, boatman, s s Howard, 1st e Jefferson

Leddy, W D, saloon, 43 Pine, res 135 Monroe

Ledvina, Joseph, grocer, 407 Main, res the same

Ledwith, Nellie Miss, res s s Chicago, 2d e Clay

Leeson, Wm, laborer, res w s Webster, 2d s Doty

Lee, Jay, laborer, w s Jefferson, 2d n Doty

Lefebvre, J B, shoemaker, w s Adams, 4th n Pine, res the same

Lefebvre' J, shoemaker, w s Adams, 4th n Pine, res the same

LEFEBVRE, L, flour and feed, n s Main, 2d e Beaumount House, res se cor Webster and Main

Leglise, Desire, s s Pine, 3d e Monroe

Legross, Daniel, carpenter, res s s Mason, 1st e Adams

Lewert, H, shoemaker, e s Washington, 2d s Stuart

Lehman, A.C, private school, school and res s e cor Monroe and Chicago

Lehman, Marcus, clothing, 111 Washington, res n s Walnut, 2d w Jackson

Lemarr, —, flour and feed, Washington, res 2d n Main, w s Adams

Lemieux, Joseph, carpenter. res 284 Madison

Lemons, John, clerk, 155 and 157 Washington, res sw cor
Crooks and VanBuren
Lempereur, Frederick, laborer, res se cor Cherry and Clay
Lemson, Forest, painter, res 48 Walnut
Lenay, Chas, laborer, 211 Adams
Leonard, J H, clerk, 138 Washington
Leutzen, A, bds Beaumont House
Lenz, Franklin, grocer, 174 and 176 Washington, res ne cor
Pine and Madison
Lepier, Geo, sailor, res w s Madison, 2d n Elm
LESAGE, JOSEPH, blacksmith, n s Main, 3d e Adams, res
nw cor Monroe and Crooks
Levi, Moses, peddler, res 190 Walnut
Levasseur, Rev L, minister at French Presbyterian Church
Lewis, William, cooper, res s s Main, 3d w Mason
Lewis, John, shingle agent, res se cor Cedar and Clay
LIBBEY, OLIVER, insurance agent, office, 2d story 122
Washington
Lidell, Louisa, chambermaid, Beaumont House
Liebzeit, Christian, laborer, res n s Stuart, 4th e Twelfth
Liesch, Joseph, groceries and provisions, ne cor Main and
Quincy, res the same
Liesch, Joseph Jr, clerk, Joseph Leisch, res the same
Liesch, Conrad, tailor, res e s VanBuren, 1st s Stuart
Liesse, Celestin, steamboat engineer, res 39 Madison
Liesse, August, laborer, res 39 Madison
Liesse, Gustof, carpenter, res 39 Madison
Lies, John, res 363 Adams
Leinberg, Gus, clerk, bds 263 Adams
Lindley, Samuel, saw repairer, 39 Pine, res 139 Monroe
Lindsay, A M, scaler, res nw cor Jefferson and Willow
LINDSLEY, M P, real estate, cor Pine and Adams, res 266
Adams
Lindsley, Thales, res 266 Adams
Lindner, Edward, cigar-maker, 44 Pine, bds Whittington
House
Leinehan, Miss Maggie, compositor Gazette office, res Ft
Howard
Lindford, Wm, laborer, res s s Walnut 2d e Quincy
Lintelman, August, saloon keeper, e s Adams 4 s Main
Lintuer, Gottleib, elevator, res n s Cherry, 1st e Twelfth
Linzie, Frank, laborer, bds se cor Crooks and Twelfth
Lison, Isadore, insurance ag't, res s s Main, 4th e Adams
Lison, Ernest, clerk, D Butler & Son, res s s Main, 4th e
Adams
Lison, Watson, student, res s s Main, 4th e Adams

Loaff, Herman, carpenter, e s Quincy, 2d n Crooks
Lobdill, J J, lake captain, res n s Cherry, 2d e Webster
Lochmans, John, res e s Quincy, 1st s Doty
Lochmans, J J, traveling ag't, res e s Quincy, 1st s Doty
Lochman, August, carpenter, res w s Jefferson, 2d s Stuart
Lochman, T, proprietor East River House, s s Mason, 1st e
   River
Lockwood, C D. clerk, under Beaumont House, res n s
   Cherry, 1st w Eleventh
Loy, J F, attorney, office 2d story 117 Washington, res w s
   VanBuren, 1st s Cass
Lohna, Henry, laborer, res 73 Elm
Long, Sarah Mrs, washing, rear Shaylor's blk
Long, L H, telegraph operator, 107 Washington, bds nw cor
   Pine and Monroe
Looz, John, laborer, 94 Washington, res se cor Cedar and
   Clay
Louis, Felix, laborer, res n s Chicago, 1st e Twelfth
Louts, Chas, sewing machine ag't, res 222 Adams
Lower, Peter, laborer, 300 Adams
Lucas, James, shingle manufacturer, res 192 Main
Luckenbach, M, saloon keeper, n s Main, 3d w Twelfth, res
   the same
Ludwig, Daniel, carpenter, res 144 Quincy
Ludwig, Frank, cigar-maker, 44 Pine, bds 144 Quincy
Lumaye, Joseph Jr, tailor, n s Walnut, 4th w Eleventh
Lumaye, Joseph, tailor, n s Walnut, 4th w Eleventh
Lund, Jens, painter, ne cor Crooks and Baird
Luraman, Thos, painter, res e s Monroe, 2d n Chicago
Lurquin, T, grocer, sw cor Main and Adams, res Ft Howard
Lutz, Fred, grocer, 85 Washington, res Doty nr E River
Lyman, A A, boatman, res 202 Walnut

M

Maa, Thos, laborer, gas works
Maasz, Fred, mason, res s s Doty, 1st w Eleventh
Maasz, Wm, tanner, res s s Doty, 1st w Eleventh
Macabee, Frank, carpenter, res e s Jefferson, 3d n Cass
Maccau, Joseph, clerk, bds Waterloo House
Macon, Joseph, clerk, bds Bodart House
Mack, Mary, e s Monroe, 2d n Stuart
Madison, Wm, clerk, Fox River House, cor of Cherry, and
   Washington
Madison St M E Church, ne cor Madison and School
Magulpin, Geo, laborer, res 71 Elm
Mahana, Mary, e s Madison 3d n Crooks

Mahn, Theodore, tailor, res 388 Pine
Mahn, Theodore, saloon, 41 Pine
Makeague, Wm, mill-right, n s Willow, 1st w Madison
Malory, John, bill-poster, bds s s Elm, 2d w Madison
Manahan, James, laborer, s s Elm, 1st e Jefferson
Mannebach, John, shoemaker, res n s Cherry, 4th e Clay
MANNEBACH, HERBERT, boiler maker, res n s Cherry, 4th e
    Clay
Mannebach, Jacob, shoemaker, res n s Cherry, 2d w Clay
Mann, Gustoff, carpenter, res 300 Cedar
Manglas, Chas, laborer, s s Doty, 1s e Twelfth
Manning, Mary Miss, milliner, 148 Washington, bds Whit-
    tey House
March, Miss Leda, teacher in Pine st school
Mariy, F, carpenter, res nw cor Cedar and Eleventh
Marshall, S G, lumber dealer, bds Beaumont House
Marshall, L M, lumber dealer, res Ft Howard
Marshall, J S, boot and shoe dealer, 138 Washington, res Ft
    Howard
Martin, Eli, real estate and N P, 81 Washington, res e s Mill
    2d s Crooks
Martin, Della, nw cor Madison and Lawe st
Martin, Emis, laborer, e s Adams, 5th s Cass
Martin, Joseph, shingle packer, e s Adams, 5th s Çass
Martin, Willie, shingle packer, e s Adams, 5th s Cass
Martin, Alex, carpenter, res w s Jackson, 2d n Crooks
Martin, E, land ag't, 81 Washington, res e s Madison, 2d s of
    Crooks
MARTIN, M L, attorney, office 2d story 242 Washington, res
    w s Monroe, bet Eliza and Emilie
Martin, M L Jr, treasury department G B & M R R, res e s
    Monroe, bet Eliza and Emilie
Martin, Leonard, U S Engineer, res e s Monroe, bet Eliza
    and Emilie
MARTIN, XAVIER, real estate, 81 Washington, res ne cor
    Monroe and Chicago
Martin, C H, printer, Gazette office, bds Adams House
Martin, F, butcher, bds ne cor Pine and Adams
Martin, May, tailoress, s s Cherry, 1st n Fox River House,
    bds Mrs Dickenson's, Adams
Martin, Mary C Mrs, wid, res 34 Main
Martens, John, hardware, s s Main, 3d w Adams, res e s
    Adams, 2d n Doty
Marchand, P, physician, res se cor Cherry and Adams
March, Mary, 133 Cherry
Marshall, Joseph, laborer, res 300 Madison

Marshall, Tato, laborer, res 300 Madison
Marshall. L M, boots and shoes, 138 Washington, res Ft
   Howard
Marshall, J S, clerk, Marshall & Dawlins, res 213 Monroe
Martel, Joseph, E River Brewery
Markle, Geo, harness maker, 89 Washington, res 91 Main
Markert, G, blacksmith, H White, bds Bay City House
Martin, C H, printer, Gazette office, bds Adams House
Mass, Laura, 191 Adams
Marks, Nicholas, laborer, ne cor Quincy and Pine
MARVIN, W H, upholsterer and furniture, 98 Washington,
   bds 221 Adams
MARVIN. H, printer, Gazette office, bds Adams House
MASSE, JOHN B, clerk of Court, and Consul of Belgium,
   res nw cor Quincy and Eliza
Masse, C, engineer, res 39 Monroe
Masonic Hall, 3d story Whitney blk
MATILE, G E, attorney and court commissioner, 109 Wash-
   ington, bds 1st National Hotel
Matile, James, printer, Gazette office, bds 17 School
Matto, Addie, waitress, Beaumont House
Matto, Mary, 69 Cherry
Matz, August, farmer, s s St Clair, 1st e Baird
Maxwell, C B, assistant freight ag't, G B & M R R, res se
   cor Walnut and Madison
May, Geo, mason, res n s Walnut, 1st w Clay
McBride, M, hostler, s s Pine, 1st e Adams
McBride, John, laborer, res 176 Pine
McCann, Ann Mrs, wid, res se cor Washington and Crooks
McCarthy, Chas, tailor, 101 Washington, bds 1st National
   Hotel
McCormick, Mary Mrs, wid, res 265 Jefferson
McCormick, Michael, book-keeper, Monitor Iron Works, res
   265 Jefferson
McCormick, Pat, drayman, res 160 Pine
McCormick, Thomas, res 105 Main
McCorrick, John, apprentice Green Bay Tannery, bds Tre-
   mont House
McClaughlin, Jas, bds U S Hotel
McClusky, Philip, laborer, s s Mason, 2d w Eleventh
McCue, Mary A, res n s Walnut, 3d e Eleventh
McCuen, John, saw-filer, s s Pine, 3d w Eleventh
McCugh, T, well borer, bds Minnesota House
McCugh. J, Cook, bds Minnesota House
McDonald, Pat, saloon, sw cor Adams and Cass
McDonald, Mary, 211 Adams

McDonald, Wm, student, bds Fox River House
McDONNELL, J, architect, 47 Washington, res Ft Howard
McDonnell, J H, Student, 47 Washington, res Ft Howard
McDonnell, Pat, saloon, se cor Cass and Adams, res s s Cass,
　2d e Adams
McDonough, Anthony, shoe dealer, 110 Washington, res e s
　Quincy, 2d e Pine
McDevit, Sadie, sw cor Crooks and Jackson
McDevit, Frederick, passenger conductor, C & N W R R,
　res s s Crooks. 2d w Jackson
McFAYDEN, MRS J, milliner and fancy goods, 116 Washing-
　ton, res sw cor Main and Quincy
McFayden, F. cor Main and Quincy
McFlynn, John. hostler, cor Washington and Walnut, bds 44
　Walnut
McGee, Mrs E C, res 124 Walnut
McGinnis, Ann, 266 Adams
McGrath, Michael. gas fitter, se cor Eleventh, and St Clair
McKabe, Lizzie 96 Main
McLean, Pat. teamster. res sw cor Doty and Clay
McNanee, R, express messenger, W C R R
McNamara, John, shoemaker, cor Pine and Washington, bds
　Whittington House
McQuade, Mary, nw cor Jefferson and Doty
McQuaig, Michael. laborer. res w s Quincy, 2d s Walnut
McTagert, Daniel, 283 Monroe
Meade, M J, county clerk, res w s Monroe. 2d n Crooks
M E Church. ne cor Madison and School
M E, Church, (German.) n s Doty, bet Adams and Jefferson
Medherst, Mary Mrs. wid. bds w s VanBuren, 1st n Stuart
Mee, Thomas, in gas works, res s s Willow, 1st e Jefferson
Mee, John, foreman gas works, res 100 Washington
Mee. John. gas fitter. bds Minnesota House
Meehen, Bridget. w s Madison. 4th s Stuart
Mellen, W S, res cor Kellogg and Cherry Ft Howard
Melzer, Mary, 188 Mason
Melzer, Louisa, nw cor Cherry and Monroe
Menrion, G, 66 Quincy
Menny, Florence Miss, res sw cor Mason and Goodell
Merimack, Sarah seamstress, res w s Jackson, 2d n Stuart
Mericle, G. turner. bds Minnesota House
Merilemans, L, grocer. n s Main 1st e Beaumont, res same
Metz, Wm, tanner, n s Doty. 2d e Twelfth
Meyer, Christian, filer. s s Pine, 3d e Clay
Meyer, Nicholas. mason, res n s Walnut, 2d e VanBuren
Meyer, Nicholas, laborer, s s Crooks 1st e Twelfth

Meyers, Frank, carpenter, bds 275 Main
Meyer, Crara, se cor Jefferson and Walnut
Mielan, Eureka, bds Adams House
MICHAAL, A, jeweler, 29 Pine, res 160 Walnut
Miller, Henry, groceries, cor Doty and Eleventh, res same
Miller, Henry, 2d bar-tender, Beaumont House
Miller, Chas, teamster, n s Cedar, 3d w Twelfth
Miller, Edward, carpenter, res n s Elm, 1st w Twelfth
Miller, John, carpenter, e s Jackson, 2d n Crooks
Miller, Harriet, 283 Monroe
Miller, Mathew, house mover, res ne cor Jefferson and Cass
Miller, John, civil engineer, res 290 Jefferson
Miller, Peter, teamster, res 294 Jefferson
Miller, Jacob, res 370 Adams
Miller, F, barber, bds Fox River House
Miller, Chas, shoemaker, bds U S Hotel
Miller, Lottie, res s s Cherry, 3d e Fox River House
Miles, R A Mrs, wid, res e s Madison, 2d n Crooks
Minnesota House, n s Main, bet Adams and Jefferson
Mister, Christian, carpenter, res s s Cherry, 3d w Eleventh
Mister, Ernest, carpenter, res s s Cherry, 3d w Eleventh
Mister, Chas, carpenter, res s s Cherry, 3d w Eleventh
Mitchell, R, yard-master, W C R R, bds 88 Pine
Mix, Chas E, fish and oysters, res n s Pine, 2d e VanBuren
Mix, Isaac C, fish and oysters, res n s Pine, 2d e VanBuren
Moger, Josie Miss, bds nw cor Pine and Jackson
Moger, John, dealer in staves, res e s Jackson, 3d n Mason
Moger, Wm R, dealer iu staves, res e s Jackson, 3d n Mason
Mohn, J A, shoemaker, res n s Main, 3d e VanBuren
Mohr, Edward, clerk, res 279 Adams
Mohr, Louis, clerk, 122 Washington, res 279 Adams
Mollitor, Philip, clerk, J S Barker 31 Pine, bds 47 Main
Moneghan, Jas, laborer, res s s Elm, 1st e of Adams
Monroe, A, physician, nw cor Pine and Jackson
Monroe, |Frederick, shoemaker, ne cor Main and VanBuren
Moravian Church, s s Moravian
Moraux, Victor, clerk, 81 Washington, res n s Willow, city
    limits
Moran, Elizabeth, 174 Main
Morenn, E, barber, 17 School
Morell, Elijah, barber, 47 Cherry, bds 283 Monroe
Morell, Jas, bds e s Madison, 1st s Mason
Morrell, Jas, shingle packer, bds Fox River House
Morrell, Hugh, bds e s Madison, 1st s Mason
Morrill, L, propriztor saloon, 151 Washington
Moritz, Kate, 174 Cherry

Morgan, Bonnie, e s Washington, 5th s Stuart
Morris, Jane, nurse, Beaumont House
Morris, Joseph, carpenter, res 42 Doty
Morris, Boswell, res 358 Jefferson
Morris, J R, city clerk's office, res 358 Jefferson
Morrow, Elisha, res nw cor Crooks and Adams
Mossler, Catherine Mrs, n s Quincy, 3d n Chicago
MUELLER, THEO, dry goods, 103 Washington, res 162
  Walnut
Mueller, August, carpenter, res se cor Stuart and Washington
Munroe, J A, clerk, gen freight office, G B & M R R, bds n
  w cor Pine and Monroe
Murphy, Mary, 156 Main
Muskosh, Mary, 225 Jefferson

N

Nau, L, grocer, 150 Washington, res Adams
Nau, Albert, merchant, res se cor Adams and Doty
National Bank of Commerce, cor Washington and Pine, G
  A Lawton, pres't, E Decker, cashier
Nathan, R W, gen passenger ag't, G B & M R R, office
  Shaylor blk
Neble, Ernest, carpenter, res s s St Claire, 2d e Baird
Neese, L, books and music, 122 Washington, res cor Mason
  and Jefferson
Negedlo, John, laborer, n s Elm, 2d e St George
Neilson, Hans, foundryman bds 239 Main
Neilson, Annie, w s Quincy, bet Mason and Cass
Nelson, S, veterinary surgeon, Harrimans barn
Nelson, Annie, 192 Main
Nelson, John, cook, Beaumont House
Netter, Louis, druggist, 49 Main, res w s Main, 1st n Doty
Netter, Adolph, clerk, Netter & Kieth, res w s Main, 1st n
  Doty
Neumann, William, tailor, res n s Stuart, 6th e Clay
Neumann, Fred, mason, se cor Stuart and Eleventh
Neubauer, F, butcher, 158 Washington, bds same
Neufelt, P, tailor, 25 Cherry, bds Green Bay House
NEVILLE, JOHN, attorney, office over Bank of Commerce,
  res nw cor Main and Madison
NEVILLE, ARTHUR, attorney, office over Bank of Com-
  merce, res e s Webster 1st n Chicago
Nevins, John H, machinist, bds 139 Monroe
Newton, Jennie, waitress, Beaumont House
Newell, Chas, carpenter, res w s Monroe, 3d s Chicago
Newcombe, C D, bds 176 Madison

New York Saloon, M Risch, proprietor, 107 Washington
Nichols, J P, carpenter, res n s Cherry, 3d w Eleventh
NICHOLS, ROB'T, lumberman, ne cor Cedar and Clay, res n
s Cherry, 1st e Eleventh
Nicholson, D E Mrs, wid, res 186 Madison
Nicholas, Wm, res ne cor Jefferson and Cass
Nick, John, carpenter, ne cor Walnut and Eleventh
Nick, Joseph, shoemaker, n s Walnut, 3d e bridge, res e s
Monroe, 2d s Doty
Niegar, Adolph, mason, 369 Walnut
Nitz, Alvina, w s Jefferson, 2d s Pine
Noehle, Theo, variety store and green house, cor Pine and
Jefferson, res w s Jefferson, 2d s Pine
Nohr, Augusta, 211 Adams
Nordhous, Chas, laborer, res e s St George, 3d n Elm
Nordhous, Henry, laborer, res e s St George, 3d n Elm
Norris, W H, attorney, res 364 Adams
Norris, J M, auditor, G B & M R R Co, office Shaylor's blk,
res sw cor Howard and Madison
Northam, J V, wholesale liquor, 149 Washington, res ne cor
Cherry and Quincy
Northam, Barthena Mrs, wid, res ne cor Cherry and Quincy
Northwestern Life Insurance Co, H Geeseler, ag't, No 60
Washington
North, Geo, clerk, Robinson's book store, res e s Madison, 3d
n Crooks
North, Ceylon, res e s Madison, 3d n Crooks
Norwach, Jacob, laborer, res 357 Walnut
Notting, John, painter, res s s Cherry, 3d e Fox River House
Nys, Mary, s s Doty, 2d w Quincy
Nys, Peter, laborer, res s s Elm, 2d e Twelfth
Nys, Louis, laborer, res s s Elm, 2d e Twelfth

O

O'Brien, Rev Jas, assistant pastor cathedral, res adjoining
South
O'Conor, Patrick grocer, 205 Walnut, res same
O'Conor, Mary, nw cor Jefferson and Doty
Oldenburg, August, res e s St George, 2d n Elm
O'Leary, Humphrey, O'Leary's boiler works, Ft Howard,
res 198 Main
O'Leary, Daniel, boiler maker, res 198 Main
O'Leary, Timothy, boiler maker, res 198 Main
O'Leary, Wm, dispatch bearer with D. M. Kelley, res 198
Main

O'Leary. Michael, boatman, res 198 Main
O'Leary, John, boiler-maker, res 198 Main
O'Leary. Humphrey Jr, boiler-maker, res 198 Main
OLMSTED, A F, physician, res sw cor Adams and Cherry, office 1st w
Opera House, Geo, Crikelair manager, n s Cherry, bet Adams and Jefferson
Orth, John, shoemaker, res 65 Chicago
OTT, H J, jeweler, 134 Washington, res s s Crooks, 2d w Madison
Otto, Alvina, n s Walnut, 1st w Quincy

P

Paderson, Miss Sarah E, teacher, 1st ward Primary
Pahl, A, furniture, 159 Washington, res 201 Walnut
Pardee, A E, jeweler, 108 Washington, res 2d story 110 and 112 Washington
Parento, Abraham, res s s Mason, 1st e Adams
Parent, John, teamster, res 358 Main
Parish, W, hides, rags and furs, 144 Washington, res nw cor Quincy and Mason
Parish School, nr Christ Episcopal Church
Parish, Porter, res 334 Jefferson
Parish, L, clerk, 146 Washington, res 334 Jefferson
Parker, Miss Julia, clerk 127 Washington, bds H D Bannisters
Parker, Frank, mason, bds Fox River House
Parmentier, J, s s Main, 4th n Adams, bds Bodart House
Parks, R G, res nw cor Pine and Monroe
Patterson, David, cistern builder, res n s Cedar, 2d w Monroe
Paul, A, cabinet-maker, res 201 Walnut
Paul, Jacob, laborer, res s s Cedar, 4th e St George
Peak, C B Mrs, wid, res e s Jefferson, 2d n Crooks
Peak, M D, Cashier, 1st National Bank, 126 Washington, res ne cor Jefferson and Stuart
PEARCE. H, physician. office, s s Cherry, 1st w of Adams, res sw cor Quincy and Congress
Pearse. Anton, plasterer, res 270 Crooks
Pear, Felix. night-watchman, res nw cor Jackson and Crooks
Pease, Miss, Lydia, res w s Jefferson, 2d n Doty
Pease, Loran, clerk, bds se cor Chicago and VanBuren
Peetsch, Chas, civil engineer, G B & M R R, office Shaylor's blk, bds cor Pine and Jefferson
Peck, W, res se cor Elm and Twelfth
Pelkin, J P, laborer, res s e cor Cedar and Quincy
Pelkin. Alex, laborer, res se cor Cedar and Quincy

Pennings, John, laborer, res s s Elm, 4th e St George
Percy, Geo T, druggist, 119 Washington, res nw cor Cherry and VanBuren
Perkins. Jas G, music teacher, res s s Pine, 2d n Clay
Perlet. D, carpenter, res s s Walnut, 3d e Clay
Pero, Felix, res 34 Clay
Perow, Flora, tailoress, s s Cherry, 1st e Fox River House, res 34 Clay
Perow. Jos, clerk. No 47 Main, bds same
Peters, Florence. cook, Beaumont House
Peterson, W H freight ag't, res 377 Adams
Petersen, L, laborer, w s Monroe, 2d n Crooks
Petersen, Peter, laborer, res 227 Quincy
Peterson, James. carriage-maker, n s Walnut, 1st e City Hotel, res Ft Howard
Peterson, Chas. mason, bds Minnesota House
Peter, Mary, e s Washington. 3d s Stuart
Pettibone, W C, merchant, res sw cor Cherry and Madison
PETRY, FRED, shoemaker, res 194 Walnut
Pfaff, A, organ tuner, 151 Washingtou. bds same
Pfeiffer, Frederick, sewing machine ag't, res n s Walnut, 3d e Clay
Pfeiffer, Dora Mrs, wid, res n s Walnut, 3d e Clay
Pfeiffer, Nicholas, carpenter, res n s Stuart, 3d w Eleventh
PFOTENHAUER, CHAS, saloon, ne cor Main and Adams, res ne cor Cedar and Twelfth
Pfotenhauer, Herman, proprietor saloon. s s Cherry, bet Washington and Adams,
Pierner, Wm, laborer, res nw cor Main and Eighth
Pierraid, Joseph, shoemaker, res nw cor Elm and Monroe
Pies, Frank, res n s Doty, 1st e Twelfth
Pigion, Peter, clerk, res 338 Main
Pigion, Zera. laborer, res 78 Elm
PINTO. J A, grocer, 110 Washington, res s s Crooks, 3d w Jackson
PINTO, WM, grocer. 110 Washington, res s s Crooks, 3d w Jackson
Pinto. A M, book-keeper, res s s Crooks, 3d w Jackson
PINTO, SAMUEL, grocer, 110 Washington. res s s Crooks. 3d w Jackson
Piraux, Frank. proprietor East River Brick yard, res s s Polier nr Suydam
Phelps, J R. mason. res s s Pine, 2d w Eleventh
Phelps, W E. mason, res s s Pine. 2d w Eleventh
Phiel, Fred. mason, bds Bay City House
Phillips, E A. laborer, res n s Cedar. 1st w Quincy

Plantekow, J, saloon, s s Cherry, 4th e Fox River House, bds Adams House
Plessing, C F, jeweler, n s Main, bet Adams and Jefferson
Plunkett, Mrs, wid, res se cor Pine and Monroe
Plunkett, John A, proprietor saloon, 151 Washington
Poirier, Isidore, res n s Main, 3d e Clay
Poirier, Edwin, carpenter, res n s Main, 3d e Clay
Poirier, M L, rooms 97 Washington
Polachek, T, tinsmith, res city limits
Polish Roman Catholic Church, n s Crooks, bet Twelfth and Baird
Pond, C M, attorney, 2d story, 120 Washington. bds w s Adams, 3d s of Walnut
Popke, Michael, laborer, res e end Eliza nr Goodell
Poten, J H, laborer, res n s Crooks, 2d e Eleventh
Poten, J H Jr, harness-maker, res n s Crooks, 2d e Eleventh
Potier, T, laborer, res sw cor Eleventh and Cedar
Potier, C, shoemaker, 112 Washington
Potter, A E, civil engineer, res No 1 Spring
Potz, John, foundryman, res n s Doty, 4th e Twelfth
Powers, John, blacksmith, res e s Jefferson, 3d s Mason
Preble' Rob't J, ship carpenter, res 206 Cherry
Predblaus, Fred, hostler, City Hotel
Primley, Rob't horses and cattle dealer, res e s Eleventh, 2d n Pine
Primmer, Eliza Mrs, wid, res sw cor Walnut and Twelfth
Prince, Fanny Mrs, wid, res sw cor Elm and Twelfth
Pritchard, Lizzie, 295 Monroe
Proctor, Frank, lumberman, bds Fox River House
Proswoskis, F, furnaceman, G B Iron Co
Proschek, Frank, book-keeper, res n s Cherry, 2d e Eleventh
Protestant Episcopal Church, (St James,) se cor Monroe and Lawe
Provancher, Ludyer, blacksmith, bds 365 Main
Public School, 3d ward, ne cor Twelfth and Elm
Public School, 2d ward, s s VanBuren, 2d n Cherry
Public School, 1st ward, se cor Madison and Chicago
Puets, T J, proprietor Union Mills, res s w cor Doty and Twelfth
Puerner, Wm, shoemaker, res cor Main and Quincy
PUGH, JOHN D, carpenter, res se cor Cedar and Twelfth
Pukall, Minnie, w s Monroe 2d n Cherry

Q

Quigley, Thomas, laborer, res s s Mason, 1st w Eleventh
Quigley, M, laborer, res n s Mason, 1st e Cherry

R

Radcliffe, Arthur, printer, Advocate office, bds Whittington House

Radtke, Lena, e s VanBuren, 2d s Mason

Ragart, Frederick, section boss, res w s Jackson, 3d s Grignon

Rahn, Henry, proprietor East River Brewery, Main, e Twelfth, res same

RAISKY, F, music teacher, res s s Main, 4th e Adams

Raisky, Nettie, dress-maker, n s Main, 4th w Jefferson, res s s Main, 4th e Adams

Raisky, Rosa, dress-maker, n s Main, 4th w Jefferson, res s s Main, 4th e Adams

Rank, T, barkeeper, Bay City House

Ranous, Geo E, contractor, res s s Cherry, 1st e of Jefferson

Ranous, Jas E, conductor, N W R R, res s s Cherry, 1st e of Jefferson

Ranous, E J, news boy, G B & M R R, res s s Cherry, 1st e of Jefferson

Rappleye, H J, machinist, res 376 Main

Rasmussen, Lena, res sw cor Cherry and Madison

Rasmussen, Otto D, clerk, 103 Washington, bds Bay City House

Rash, Abram, teamster, res 22 Cedar

Rash I, res 22 Cedar

Rash, Daniel, res 22 Cedar

Rash, Wm, laborer, res 22 Cedar

Rash, Geo, laborer, res 22 Cedar

Rashki, Flora, 258 Jefferson

Rathman, Henry, cooper, res 33 Monroe

Rathman, Edward, shoemaker, res 33 Monroe

Rattinger, Chas, C, with H J Ott, bds s s Crooks, 1st w of Madison

Rawley, Frank, laborer, res 128 Jefferson

Raymakers, Peter, wagon-maker, s s Walnut. 4th e of Eleventh

Reamich, Mathew, barber, s s Cherry, 4th e Fox River House, res sw cor, Monroe and Moravian

Reber, Annie Mrs, wid, res 175 Cherry

Reber, Mary, compositor, G B Volks Zietung office, bds 175 Cherry

Redline, Jos S, shingle dealer, res e s Adams, 3d n of Main

Redeman, C W, proprietor Bay City House, cor Washington and Walnut

Regutt, Henry, shoemaker, 110 Washington, bds City Hotel

Rehder, Hannah, chambermaid, City Hotel

Reid, James, laborer, bds se cor St Claire and Eleventh
Reinke, G, proprietor Bear saloon, 83 Washington, res same
Reis, Anton, bar tender, Reis's Hotel, res the same
Reis, Loenard, butcher, s s Main, 1st e Green Bay House, res
    339 Adams
Reis, Andrews, proprietor Reis's Hotel, s s Main, 2d w
    Eleventh,
Rentmuster, Andrew, laborer, e s Jefferson, 3d s Mason
Renier, Eugene, res s s Mason, 3d w of Goodell
Resch, John, saloon, res s s Pine, 2d e Quincy
Resch, M, proprietor New York saloon, 107 Washington, res
    150 Jefferson
Revet, Lizzie, kitchen girl, Beaumont House
Reynolds, A H, books and stationary, 48 Pine, bds 159 Main
Reynolds, Worden, res e s Webster, 1st n Chicago
Rhoda, Anna, laundress, Beaumont House
Rhode, H, physician. res 144 Jefferson
Rhoda, Cecilia, laundress, Beaumont House
Rhody. Wm, wagon-maker, bds e s Jefferson, 2d s Walnut
Rice, Henry, carpenter, s s Walnut, 1st w Clay
Richardson, A W, teamster, res n s Walnut, 2d e Eleventh
Richard. Albert, bds w s Twelfth, 1st n Elm
Richie, James, lumber yard, ne cor Cedar and Day res DePere
Richie, Joshua, laborer, res 177 Walnut
Richie, Wm, porter, res 177 Walnut
Richman, I. clothier, 111 Washington, bds Beaumont House
Rider, Miss Mary J, teacher, res cor VanBuren and Grignon
Ringer. Gerald, laborer, res s s Doty, 2d e Twelfth
Risch, Peter, res n s Cherry, 2d e Quincy
Risch, Chas, freight marker, res n s Cherry, 2d e Quincy
Ritter, Barbara Mrs, wid, res n s Cedar, 4th e St George
RIVARD, H, proprietor national saloon, 97 Washington, res
    same
Robb, James. res ne cor Monroe and Polier
Roberts, Miss M L. proprietor ice cream saloon, 43 Cherry,
    res same
ROBERTS, M E, proprietor livery stable, e end Walnut st
    bridge, saloon and res 2d e bridge
Roberts, Chas, foundryman, bds St Louis House
Robinson, J W, carpenter, res sw cor Pine and Webster
Robinson, J. druggist, cor Pine and Washington, res 141
    ·Walnut
Robinson, Richard, clerk, VanNostrand, Klaus & Co, bds
    141 Walnut
ROBINSON, A C, proprietor Green Bay Advocate, 36 Pine,
    res 409 Lawe

ROBINSON, C D, proprietor Green Bay Advocate, 36 Pine. res 409 Lawe

Robinson, T, druggist, cor Washington and Pine, res Manitowoc

Robinson, G, proprietor Fox River House, cor Cherry and Washington

Roach, Herman L, 1st bar tender, Beaumont House

Rock, Chas T, trunk maker, e s Washington, 3d s Doty, bds Fox River House

Roe, Richard, sailor, res n s Walnut, 1st w Twelfth

Roe, James, sailor, res 106 Cedar

Roe, Henry, sailor, res 106 Cedar

Roffz, John, miller, bds at Whittington House

Rogalski, Henry, brickmaker, res w s Goodell, 1st s Porlier

Rogers, Oscar, blacksmith, e s Adams, 3d s Main, res w s Madison, 2d s Elm

Rondon, F Z, teacher, res 320 Jefferson

Rondon, Francis, res 320 Jefferson

Rohn, John, res sw cor Cherry and Quincy

Rohn, Jas, laborer, res sw cor Cherry and Quincy

Root, Chas H, tinner, 162 Washington, res s s Doty, 2d e of Monroe

Root, Erastus, printer and binder, 122 Washington, res n s Cherry, 3d e of Quincy

Root, Harrison, laborer, n s Cherry, 3d e Twelfth

Root, Jos, bell boy, Beaumont House

Roof, Joseph, painter, res basement Turner Hall

Rose, Geo W, passenger conductor, G B & M R R, res se cor Monroe and Doty

Rose, Rudolph, laborer, res n s Porlier, 1st w Baird

Rothe, Carl, carpenter, res 96 Twelfth

Rosmanlen, Peter, clerk, W M Bruce & Co, Ft Howard, res n s Monroe, 2d n Chicago

Rosmanlen, Frank, sewing machine ag't, res ne cor Walnut and VanBuren

Rosenauer, J, barkeeper, 151 Washington, bds same

Rothe, Wm, wagon maker for Weise

Rosso, Frederick, bds e s Jefferson, 2d n Lawe

Rossiter, Mrs M, w s Jefferson, 2d n Doty

Rossiter, Kate, w s Jefferson, 2d n Doty

Roulet Sandy, drayman, res s s Elm, 2d w Madison

Roulet, Alex, cook, res s s Elm, 2d w Madison

Routledge, J B, express messenger, G B & L S route

Royoke, August, laborer, res e s Jackson, 1st s Emilie

Roy, M A, groceries and liquors, res ne cor Jefferson and Milwaukee

18

Roznowski, John, foundryman, res s s Stuart, 4th e Twelfth
Rubesson, Peter, laborer, w s Quincy, bet Mason and Cass
Rudden, Mary, 203 Adams
Ruebenkoenig, J, shoemaker, Blosh & Co, bds Green Bay
House
Rukamp, Henry, laborer, bds nw cor Cedar and Twelfth
Rummel, Adam, carpenter, res w s Quincy, 1st n Walnut
Rummel, Andrew, printer, Root & Kimball, res w s Quincy,
1st s Walnut
Rummel, Lena, compositor, Wis Staats Zietung, res w s
Quincy, bet Walnut and Doty
Rush, John, carpenter, res se cor Crooks and Twelfth
Rush, Frederick, laborer, s s Porlier, 1st e Twelfth
Rutledge, John B, express messenger, res 249 Pine
Rynier, Eugene, laborer, res s s Mason, 3d w Goodell

S

Safranck, John, weaver, res s s Cherry, 3d e Eleventh
Sager, Geo, C, printer, foreman Advocate office, res 162
Jefferson
Saguin, James, carpenter, res e s Madison, 1st s Mason
Saguin, William, clerk, res e s Madison, 1st s Mason
SALE, L B, attorney, 142 Washington, bds 132 Main
Sargent, S H, veterinary surgeon, res 202 Cherry
SARGEANT, C E, Sup't Green Bay Iron Works, res 141
Cherry
Sayer, Eliza Mrs, res nw cor Adams and Crooks
Schaus, P, cigar-maker, bds Bay City House
Schellenbeck, Jacob, leather dealer, n s Main, 4th e Adams,
res n s Cedar, 2d w Eleventh
Schellenbeck, Otto, clerk, Cherot & Co, res n s Cedar, 2d w
Eleventh
Scheibe, Wm, laborer, res s s Walnut, 2d w Eleventh
Scheller, Louisa, wid, res 38 Stuart
Scheller, Herman, carpenter, res 38 Stuart
Scheller, Louis, saloon, cor School and Monroe, res n s
School, 1st e Monroe
Schettler, F R, hardware, 84 Washington, res 262 Adams
Schellar, Louisa Miss, tailoress, 25 Cherry, res same
SCHETTLER, E J, agricultural impliments, s s Walnut, 2d w
Washington, res — Adams
Schettler, F R, hardware, 84 Washington, res n s Stuart, 3d
w Twelfth
Schiller, Gustoff, book-keeper, res s s Cherry, 2d w Monroe
Schiller, Louis, city brewery, res s s Stuart, 2d e Clay
Schleies, Fred, shoemaker, res w s Twelfth, 2d n Elm

Schmidt, Herman, mason, res w s Eleventh, 3d n Cass
Schmidt, Klein, laborer, res e s Monroe, 1st n Grignon
Schmidt, John,'carpenter, res s s Chicago, 1st e Eleventh
Schmidt, Annie, dining room girl, Bay City House
SCHMIDT, H, physician, office and res se cor Adams and
    Cherry
Schmiedeknecht, Wm, teamster, Bay City House, res same
Schneider, Henry, mason, res n s Walnut, 5th w Eleventh
Schneider, W, photographer, with C F Schroeder, 118
    Washington, bds with Schroeder
Schroeder, Julius, laborer, e s Quincy, 1st n Grignon
Schroeder, Chas, photographer, 118 Washington, res nw cor
    Pine and Quincy
Schraa, Barbara, 143 Monroe
Schraw, Herbert, carpenter, res s s Walnut, 2d w Clay
Schram, Julius, steamboat engineer, res s s Cedar, 1st e St
    George
Schultz, L O, clerk, ne cor Pine and Washington
Schutte, J H, laborer, res w s Jackson, 1st s Stuart
Schults, L, bds United States Hotel
Schutte, Henry, clerk, 155 Washington. bds w s Jackson, 1st
    s Stuart
Schutte, Fred, clerk, Skeeles & Best, 127 Washington
Schutte, J H, editor G Bay Volks Zeitung, res ne cor Adams
    and Stuart
Schutte, John D, foreman lumber yard, res se cor Pine and
    Clay
Schumacher, Frank, saloon and grocery, sw cor Main and
    Webster, res same
Schumacher, H, meat-market, sw cor Main and Webster, res
    same
Schumacher, Q, meat-market, sw cor Main and Webster, res
    same
Schumacher, J M, res 258 Jefferson
Schumacher, J P, upholster, e s Adams, opp Adams House
Schunzk, Chas, proprietor saloon, 153 Washington, res sw
    cor Crooks and Quincy
Schwarz, R, clerk, 105 Washington, bds se cor Chicago and
    VanBuren
Scott, Wm, real estate, res 227 Adams
Scott, Geo D, clerk, res 327 Adams
Scott, Geo, clerk, E J Schettler, s s Walnut, 2d w Washington,
    bds with Schettler
Schoeber, Leonard, cooper, res 168 Walnut
Scruton, J B. trunk manufacturer, bds Whittington House
Scruton, T L, trunk manufacturer. bds Whittington House

Scruton, Bros, trunk manufacturers, s s Washington, 3d s Doty
Schwarz, R. clerk, 105 Washington, res same
Seaveson, Emma, 124 Walnut
Seibel, Caster, n s Eleventh, 1st n Cherry
Seibel, Antoine, res w s Pine, 1st w Clay
Seibel, John, proprietor E River House, 413 Main res same
Seidel, Geo, hostler, bds cor Pine and Adams
Seger, Mary, Mrs, wid, res 176 Madison
Seger, Geo F, boots and shoes, 129 Washington, res 176 Madison
Serverson, Augusta, se cor VanBuren and Chicago
Senn, H, teacher, res n s Main, 3d e Twelfth
Servotte, Wm, carpenter, res ne cor Mason and Eleventh
Seymour, Frank, bds 221 Adams
Shay, Kate, ne cor Cass and Quincy
Shampane, Frank, w s Quincy, 2d n Grignon
Shanowa, John, carpenter, res 297 Cedar
Shaylor's Block, se cor Adams and Pine ·
Shefski, Gustoff, laborer, res e s Monroe, 2d n Grignon
Sherwood, E, res w s Madison, 1st s Porlier
Shepard, F, proprietor G B marble works, bds 1st National Hotel
Shettock, Margret, s s Pine, 1st n VanBuren
Shelley, Louis, laborer, res 119 Cedar
Sheil, Rob't, laborer, res e s Jefferson, 2d n Lawe
Shilling, N, mason, res s s Pine, 2d e Jackson
Schilling, Edward, mason, res s s Pine 2d e Jackson
Shipman, Geo, laborer, bds 275 Main
Shoemaker, Chas, laborer, res 297 Cedar
Shook, Benjamin, laborer, res 26 Monroe
Shrodt, F. shoemaker, 129 Washington
Shyern, Barbara, e s Jefferson, 2d n Crooks
Siegment, Albert, carpenter, res ne cor Doty and Clay
Silber, Robert, engineer, res 319 Adams
Siltersdorf, C, machinist, Taylor & Duncan, Ft Howard, bds Bay City House
Sills, Henry. 173 Main
Simons, Frank, laborer, bds w s Adams, 3d s Cherry
Sims, W E, express messenger, res 267 Adams
Singer, Sewing Machine, S Warn, ag't, No 170 Washington
Sisters Notre Dame, ne cor Monroe and Doty
Skarde, Matthias, tailor, res n s Main, 2d w Clay
SKEELS, M P, dry goods, 127 Washington, res n s Pine, 3d e Quincy

Skoonans, August, mason, res e s Quincy, 2d n Crooks
Slipskar, Pauline, jeweler, 132 Main
Slye, Christopher, res e s Jefferson, 2d s Cass
Smith, Albert, architect, office over Philip Klaus, Adams st,
   res 166 Quincy
Smith, Alva, res 282 Jefferson
SMITH, ALFRED, wholesale liquor, 109 Washington, res nw
   cor Cherry and Jackson
Smith, Miss Bell M, teacher in E River school
Smith, Benj H, blacksmith, res ne cor Cherry and Webster
Smith, D G, clerk, 128 Washington, res Ft Howard
Smith, D, breakman, G B & M R R, bds 143 Monroe
Smith, Fred L, sup't telegraph and train dispatcher, G B &
   M R R, bds ne cor Cherry and Jefferson
Smith, Henry, laborer, res 254 Crooks
Smith, Henry, mason, res nw cor Doty and Twelfth
Smith, Jas H, steamboat engineer, res e s Quincy, 2d n Pine
Smith, John, blacksmith, res s s Doty, 8th e Twelfth
Smith, J, express messenger, C & N W R R, bds 1st
   National Hotel
Smith, Lambert, (Lambert & Sons') res n s Main, 2d e
   Jackson
Smith, Lambert, wagon-maker and blacksmith, n s Main, 2d
   e Jackson, res same
Smith, L A Miss, book-keeper, No 113 Washington, bds w s
   Jefferson, 2d s Cass
Smith, M, laborer, res s s Cherry, 5th e Clay
Smith, Mary, res s s Cherry, 5th e Clay
Smith, M, liveryman, M E Roberts, e s Walnut st bridge,
   bds with M E Roberts
Smith, Mary, e end Walnut st bridge
Smith, Peter, laborer, res 58 Elm
Smith, Rob't W E, baggage master, G B & M R R, res 40
   Madison
Smith, R H, omnibus driver, res 89 Cedar
Smith, Rockway, res nw cor Cherry and Jackson
Smits, H, blacksmith, bds U S Hotel
Solman, Jardieu, laborer, bds n s Main, 3d e Adams
Sommers, Geo, dry goods, wholesale and retail, w s Wash-
   ington, bet Main and Pine, res 300 Adams
Soper, David, proprietor saloon, 43 Pine, res w s Quincy, 3d
   s Stuart
SORENSON, B J, cabinet-maker, res s w cor Madison and
   Cass
Sorenson, S P, auction and commission merchant, 77 Wash-
   ington, res se cor Madison and Cass

Sorenson, John, clerk, 84 Washington, res 182 Madison
Spaats, Mary, 110 and 112 Washington
Spear, Thomas, ship builder, res n s Willow, 1st w St George
Spencer, Hershell, gas fitter, 90 Washington, res cor Van-
    Buren and Crooks
Spoden, Nic, sw cor Main and Jefferson bds same
Sprague, Jas, carpenter, res e s Jefferson, 1st n Spring
Spunots, Godfrey, laborer, res n s Cedar, 1st w Quincy
Sputty, John, mason, res se cor Cherry and Eleventh
Sputty, Fred, mason, res s s Doty, 7th e Twelfth
Sputty, August, mason, res s s Doty, 6th e Twelfth
Stachek, Jacob, mason, res n s Crooks, 2d w Twelfth
Stadler, Catharine, Bay City House
Stancleft, W A Miss, dress-maker, 2d story 45 Cherry, res
    same
Stanley, Blanche, sewing, s s Cedar, 1st e of Adams
Stark, Minnie, ne cor Jefferson and Stuart
Star Clothing House, Richmond & Lehman, proprietors, 111
    Washington
State Gazette Office, 33 Pine, Hoskinson & Follet proprietors
Steba, Martin, laborer, res 353 Walnut
Steinkrans, August, laborer, res n s Doty, 3d e Clay
Stievo, Celentin, laborer, res n s Elm, 1st e St George
STEPPLER, L, proprietor St Louis House, e s of Main, bet
    Adams and Jefferson
Steter, Kate, n s Walnut, 2d w Jackson
Stetter Kate, at restaurant, 40 Pine
Stevens, S P, contractor and builder, Shaylor's block, bds
    Adams House
STEVENS, J V, commission merchant, and dealer in fish, 74
    Washington, res 143 Monroe
Stevens, J V, commission merchant, 155 Adams, res 143
    Monroe
Stevenans, J B, res 71 Cedar
Stid, E, contractor, res 295 Monroe
Stock, Fred, laborer, res w s Monroe, 2d s Chicago
Stone, Jane Mrs, wid, res ne cor Cherry and Jackson
Stonbring, Wm, laborer, res s s Stuart, 7th e Twelfth
Strahl, Herman, Chicago saloon, 104 Washington, res s s
    Cedar, 2d w Eleventh
Straka, Wenzel, tanner, res n s Elm, 4th e St George
Strange, John, cooper, bds 222 Main
Strong, H S, president 1st National Bank, res 234 Jefferson
Strong, George M Mrs, private school, 239 Adams res same
Strope, Wm, foundryman, res n s Walnut, 1st w Twelfth
Stumpf, John, proprietor Queen City Resturant, 40 Pine

St Denis, John, proprietor steam laundry, Washington, res nw cor Quincy and Chicago
St Louis, J J, hardware, 113 Washington, res s s Cherry, 1st e Monroe
St Louis House, s s Main, 3d e Adams
St James Protestant Episcopal Church, se cor Monroe and Lawe
St Mary's Parish School, 150 Monroe
St Mary's Church, (German Catholic,) e s Madison, 2d n of Doty
St Johns Church, (French Catholic,) w s Milwaukee, bet Jefferson and Madison
SUELFLOHN, W J, photographer, 3d story, 148 Washington, res 261 Adams
Summerfelt, Wm, laborer, res n s Walnut, 5th e Twelfth
Sumvill, John, foundryman, res n s Mason, 2d e Clay
Sund, William, shingle sawyer, bds U S Hotel
Susmami, Elizabeth, 179 Washington
Sutton, Miss Addie, teacher, 1st ward school
Suydam, J B, surveyor, res 139 Madison
Suydam, C B, foundryman, res 139 Madison
Swartz, A, clerk, with Hoffman, bds w s Jefferson, 2d n Pine
Swartz, Chas, painter, office cor Pine and Washington
Sweeney, P, laborer, res 251 Main
Sweet, Jacob, tanner, res s s Main, 2d w Twelfth
Swenson, Lawrence L, sailor, res 309 Doty

T

Tato, M, res n s Elm, 2d w of Monroe
Taylor, T W, moulder, res s s Main, 2d e of Webster
Temperance Hall, 3d story of 142 Washington
Tellor, Rosanna, at Adams House
Templeton, A, speculator, res n s Pine, 3d e of VanBuren
Teneyck, Marshal, bricklayer, res n s Cherry, 4th w of Eleventh
Teneyck, Wm, bricklayer, res n s Cherry, 4th w of Eleventh
Tenner, J F, bar keeper, n s Pine, bet Adams and Washington st
Tennes, Mary, wid, res ne cor Main and Adams, 2d floor
Tennes, Alex, bus driver, for Hagen & Co, res 49 Main, 2d floor
Tennes, Henry, baggage man, for Hagen & Co
Tennes, John, bus driver, for Hagen & Co
Tennis, Albert, laborer, res 323 Jefferson

Tennis, Henry, laborer, res 323 Jefferson
Tennis, Leonard, fish dealer, res n s Cass, 1st e of Adams
Tesch, Amelia, cook, 35 Pine
Theas, Aug, laborer, res n s Walnut, 2d e of Twelfth
Thomas, M, laborer, bds s s Cedar, 3d w of VanBuren
Thomas, W C E, postmaster, res 258 Main
Thomas, W E, assistant post-office, res e s VanBuren, 2d s
    of Main
Thompson, Andrew, shoemaker, 112 Washington, res s s
    Cherry, bet Washington and Adams
Thompson, Benj Sr, res e s Eleventh, 3d n of Pine
Thompson, Benj Jr, laborer, res e s Eleventh, 3d n of Pine
Thompson, F W, drayman, res 613 Adams
Thompson, Jos, laborer, res 483 Main
Thompson, L, mason, res ne cor Washington and Crooks
Thompson, L C, laborer, res ne cor Crooks and Washington
Thompson, Mary, 159 Main
Thompson, Wm, detective, res s s Crooks, 2d w of Van-
    Buren
Thompson, K J, tanner, res e s Eleventh, 3d n of Pine
Thiard, Bennett, carpenter, res s s Chicago, 1st e of Clay
Thiard, Claude, carpenter, bds s s Chicago, 1st e of Clay
Thiard, John, carpenter, bds s s Chicago, 1st e of Clay
Thornton, Miss Fannie M, teacher, in Pine st school
Thorsen, Bella, ne cor Monroe and Doty
Thrall, H R, Engineer, res s s Pine, 1st w of Quincy
Thrall, P F, tug captain, res 137 Monroe
Tice, F, wagon-maker, cor Washington and Doty, bds e s of
    Washington, 3d s of Stuart
Tickler, Henry, carpenter, res s s Chicago, 1st e of Madison
Tickler, Peter, bds s s Mason, 3d w of Goodell
Tidman, Edward, store room clerk, Beaumont House
Tillman, Frank, grocer, 45 Cherry, res se cor Cherry and
    Twelfth
Tilton, Frank, editor Green Bay Advocate, res 147 Monroe
Tisdale, G J, attorney, sw cor Pine and Adams, bds Beau-
    mont House
Todd, John, stationary engineer, res w s VanBuren, 1st s of
    Stuart
Tone, Frederick, grocer, 255 Main, res 12 VanBuren
Tonean, John, brick-maker, res nw cor Mason and Goodell
Torean, Julian, brick-maker, bds nw cor Mason and Goodell
Tonisoul, Louis, mason, res 361 Adams
Toatloff, Moses, clerk, res w s Jefferson, 1st s Mason
Tooker, O A, dealer in patent rights, res e s Jackson, 1st s of
    Mason

Topeck, Mary, e s Adams, 2d s of Stuart
Topliff, Miss Ellen J, clerk, 95 Washington, bds 203 Adams
Topliff, Frank, clerk, 127 Washington, bds nw cor Pine and
  Jackson
Torsensen, Hulda, 300 Adams
Tracy, C W, commission merchant, 140 Washington, res w s
  Jackson, 1st n Lawe
Tracy, J E, tailor, 111 Washington, res Ft Howard
TRACY, J J, attorney, cor Washington and Pine, res e s
  Madison, 3d s of Crooks
Travis, Jos, fireman, bds U S Hotel
Trch, Jannes, saloon and res, n s Main, 4th e of St George
Trindle, Geo, turner, res sw cor Jefferson and Elm
Tritle, Julia, se cor Jefferson and Crooks
Trowell, Capt J W, res sw cor Monroe and Walnut
Truckey, Geo, wagon-maker, bds 367 Main
Turcotte, C, carpenter, res s s Walnut, 2d e of Clay
Turner, Mrs Sarah, wid, res nw cor Madison and Polier
Turner, H L, ship builder, res nw cor Madison and Polier
Turner Hall, nw cor Monroe and Walnut
Tyler, J S, bank clerk, bds Beaumont House
Tyler, Mrs E A, bds 96 Main
Tyler, L M, ag't C & N W R R, bds Beaumont House
Tyrrell, E L, Jeweler, 95 Washington, bds nw cor Pine and
  Jackson
Tyler, W S, clerk, nw cor Pine and Washington, bds 96
  Main

U

Ulmer, Jacob, shoemaker, shop and res, n s Main, 3d w of
  Twelfth
Umberhaum, Louis, res 34 Main, (2d story)
Union Brewery, ne cor Pine and Adams
Union School House, sw cor Pine and Adams
Unpehun, Godfried, laborer, res 272 Stuart
United States Hotel, No 40 Main st
Ursuline Academy, se cor Webster and Crooks

V

Vanable, H, proprietor United States Hotel
Vambeik, Martin, laborer, res w s Jackson, 2d n of Doty
Vanbek, John, laborer, res s s Crooks, 2d e of Clay
Vancastle, John, laborer, res nw cor Pine and Eleventh
Vancaster, Oliver, laborer, res w s Twelfth, 1st s of Stuart
Vancalster, Emil, Painter for Frank Crikelair

Vance, J B, teamster, res w s Madison, 2d s of Willow

VanDenboomen, P, fisherman, res cor Washington and Stuart

VanDenmooter, J A, grocer, store and res se cor Main and Webster

VanDeuren, Henry, laborer, res n s Crooks, 2d w of Eleventh

VanDeuren, H, engineer at Kelloggs mill, res w s Jefferson, 3d s Cedar

VanDeuren, J B, cigar maker, res w s Jefferson, 3d s of Cedar

VanDueren, G J, grocer, w s Adams, 1st s of Main, res w s Jefferson, 3d s of Cedar

VanDueren, P J, grocer, w s Adams, 1st s Main, res w s Jefferson, 3d s Cedar

VanDyke, Louis, res w s Adams, 2d n of ——

Vaness, Mary, sw cor Main and Jefferson

Vangaal, Peter, carpenter, res ne cor Walnut and VanBuren

Vanherman, Frank, harness-maker, res e s Madison, 2d n of Mason

VanHorn, G W, salesman, 129 Washington, res ne cor Madison and Crooks

Vanknaken, Arnold, carpenter, bds n s Jefferson, 4th s of Mason

Vanluey, John, laborer, res nw cor Mason and Madison

VanNorstrand, A H, merchant, 67 — 70 Washington, res w s Quincy, bet Mason and Cass

VanNorstrand, F C, coal dealer, res nw cor Cherry and Monroe

Vanstlean, Frank, county treasurer, res n s Crooks, bet Webster and Clay

Vantene, Henry, carpenter, res se cor Webster and Doty

Vanvuren, Henry, physician, res n s Chicago, 1st w of Baird

Vanvicklen, Daniel, broom-maker, res w s Adams, 1st n of River

Vanert, Henry, ostler, U S Hotel

Vary, W P, station ag't, Wis Central R R, bds 1st National Hotel

Vedigum, Angel, res sw cor Chicago and Eleventh

Veizel, Aug, painter, res s s Doty, 3d w of Eleventh

Verboomen, F, grocer, store and res n s Main, 1st e Beaumont House

Verboomen, Peter, res n s of Main, 1st e of Beaumont House

Verhaden, Geo, laborer, res s s Grignon, 1st w of Jackson

Verheyden, Alex, res w s Jefferson, 4th s of Mason

Verheyden, Jos, saloon, w s of Jefferson, 3d n of Cass

Verheyden, Mrs, Josephine, wid, w s Jefferson, 4th n of Cass

Vendertile, Josephine, No 17 School st

Vermeyer, Eli, clerk, No 105 Washington, bds Waterloo House

Vernor, H, tailor, s s Cherry, 1st e of Fox River House, res same

Venoss, Adrian, carpenter, res s s Grignon, 1st w of Eleventh

Venoss, Theodore, laborer, res s s Grignon, 1st w of Eleventh

Vieaux, Jerome, furnaceman, res w s Adams, cor Polier

Vincent, C, cabinet-maker, res and shop s s of Main, 2d w of Jefferson

Vincent, John B, res w s Jefferson, 2d s of Main

Victor Sewing Machine, Whitney & Reynolds ag'ts, 48 Pine

Vonderventen, Fred, laborer, w s Monroe, 1st s of Eliza

Vorel, Josephine, cor VanBuren ard Grignon

Vosters, Minnie, 47 Main st

Vernell, Mary, kitchen girl, Beaumont House

VROMAN, CHAS E, attorney, 142 Washington, res e s Quincy 1st s Mason

Vullengo, John, blacksmith shop, se cor Jefferson and Mason, res 1st south

Vandemosselar, J, res 2d story 79 Washington

Vunckz, A, clerk, n s Main, 2d e of Beaumont

W

Wagner, Frank, stationary engineer, bds s s Main, 1st w of Twelfth

Wagner, John, blacksmith, bds e s Jefferson, 2d s of Walnut

Wagner, John, teamster, e s of St George, 4th n Elm

Wagner, L, clerk, No 40 Pine, res Astor saloon building

Wagner, Minnie, Fox River House

Wagner, Nic, painter, s s of Pine, 2d e of Adams

Wagner, Peter, clerk, with Geo, Sommers, res No 186 Madison

Wairwright, G C, mail ag't, res se cor Mason and Monroe

Walch, Elizabeth, wid of John, res w s Adams, 2d s of River

Wald, Hubert, laborer, res se cor Main and Eleventh

Wald, John P, laborer, res se cor Main and Eleventh

Wald, John P, saw-filer, res ne cor Elm and St George

Wald, Thomas, laborer, res ne cor Main and Eleventh

Walden, Chas, tanner, res n s ——, 2d e of Eleventh

Walker, James, office clerk, Beaumont House

Walker, M H, land ag't, 148 Washington

Walker, Rev J M, res 200 Madison st

Wall, James W, joiner, res n s Cherry, 4th e of Eleventh

Walley, Jos, carpenter, res w s Monroe, 2d n Mason
Walley, Peter, carpenter, res w s Monroe, 2d n Mason
Walton, Alice, e s Monroe, 2d s of Lawe
Walwitz, Chas, painter, res w s Jackson, 1st n of Doty
Warnica, F, laborer, res n s Elm, 1st e of Twelfth
Warn, S, ag't Singer Sewing Machine Co, room No 1, 70 Washington st
Warn, Mrs S, milliner, 70 Washington st, bds Beaumont House
WARREN, A A, insurance ag't, Shaylor blk, res e s Van-Buren, 1st n of Chicago
Warren, H, ostler, s s of Pine, 1st e of Adams
WARREN, C M, commission merchant, rear of 74 Washington, res 174 Cherry
Washington, Geo, cook, N W R R Depot, res 98 Washington
Washington, Mrs Geo, ladies hair dresser, 98 Washington
Waterloo House, n s Main, bet Adams and Jefferson
Watson, Geo W, register of deeds, res 124 Walnut st
Watkins, Oliver, carpenter, res e s Madison, 2d s of Willow
Watermelon, F, laborer, res n s of Crooks, 3d e of Clay
Watzelgah, Frank, laborer, res e s St George, 1st n of Main
Weaver, H, butcher, res e s Jefferson, 3d n of Cedar
Webster Square, s s of Cass bet Madison and Monroe
Weed, S O, millright, w s Jefferson, 2d n of Chicago
Wegner, Julius, teamster, No 36 Main, e of River
Weide, Aug, laborer, res s s Chicago, 2d w of Twelfth
Weidner, Ernest, pop manufacturer, res n s Pine, 2d w of Clay
WEISE, ALBERT, carriage manufacturer, Washington nr Walnut, res e s Jefferson, 2d s of Walnut
Weise, Chas, clerk, 93 Washington, res e s Jefferson, 2d s of Walnut
WEISE, H F, crockery dealer, 93 Washington, res e s Jefferson, 2d s of Walnut
Weissmiller, John, professor of music, se cor Cherry and Quincy
Welner, A, at Queen City Restaurant
Welsh, Frank, teamster, res e s Jefferson, 3d n of Cedar
Welsh, John, furnaceman, bds 239 Main
Welsh, Thos, lumberman, bds U S Hotel
Wermyin, E, clerk and rooms, 105 Washington
WERNER, E, contractor and builder, bds East River House
Werner, H, tailor, s s Cherry, 1st e of Fox River House
Werthman, H, furrier, store and res 145 Washington
West, Frank, carpenter, res e s VanBuren, 2d n of Doty

Westman, Wm, clerk, for J J St Louis, bds Adams House
Whal, Levi, barber, res s s Cedar, 1st e of Adams
Whal, Lucy, dress-maker, res s s Cedar, 1st e of Adams
Wheelock, C B, clerk, Washington, res No 100 Jefferson
Wheelock, C L, insurance ag't, 111 Washington, res s s
    Crooks, 2d e of Jackson
Wheelock, Henry C, boiler maker, res 100 Jefferson
WHEELOCK, MISS KATE I, clerk, 48 Pine, res s s Crooks,
    2d e of Jefferson
Whidden, Mrs Lydia, res nw cor Quincy and Mason
Whitaker, Mrs E, seamstress, 144 Washington
Whitaker, J, carpenter, 144 Washington
White, C H. speculator, res s s Lawe 1st e of Jefferson
White, Frank, laborer, res nw cor Madison and Cass
White, G, laborer, res e s Cass, 1st e of Eleventh
White, Henry, res s s Walnut, 1st e of VanBuren
White, H J, blacksmith, No 188 Washington, res 831 Walnut
White. J L, mail carrier, res 90 Jefferson
White, Miss Julia, assistant principal Grammar department of
    High School
White, Mrs Mary C, res 295 Monroe
Whitney, Mrs D H, wid, res 118 Main
Whitney, D M, deputy U S Marshal, res 159 Main
Whitney, Mrs E S, wid, res 118 Main
Whitney, Henry E, books and stationary, 48 Pine, res 581
    Cherry
Whitney, Josh, res 96 Main
Whitney, Sam'l United States Engineer, bds at Beaumont
    House
Whittington, H, proprietor Whittington House, se cor Wash
    ington and Doty
Whittington House, se cor Washington and Doty
Wiers, Jacob, bds U S Hotel
WIGMAN, J H M, attorney, cor Pine and Washington, res
    cor Quincy and Cass
Wigger, Peter, boot and shoe dealer, 110 Washington
Wight, Miss Millie, teacher in Pine street school
Wilde, A shoemaker, 129 Cherry, bds U S Hotel
Williams, Benj, book-keeper, 64 and 70 Washington, res 146
    Jefferson
WILLIAMS C, proprietor of restaurant, s s Adams, bet
    Washington and Jefferson
Williams, Geo H, contractor, res n s Walnut, 2d w of
    Eleventh
WILLIAMS, H N, insurance ag't, Shaylor's blk, res s s Pine,
    2d e of Monroe

Williams, J J, superintendant ofteams at Green Bay furnace, res n s Walnut, 3d e of Eleventh

Williams, J D, book-keeper for Earl & Case, res w s Monroe, 3d n of Chicago

Willim, Andrew, cigar manufacturer, s s Cherry, 3d w of Webster

Willim, Frank Sr, s s Cherry, 3d w of Webster

Willim, Frank Jr, grocer, 232 Cherry

Williquet, Euguene, flour and feed, res 182 Cherry

Williquet, G, painter, e s of Adams, 2d s of Cherry

Wills, Lucy, dress-maker, s s Cedar, 1st e of Adams

Wills, Lee, barber, res s s Cedar, 1st e of Adams

Wilner, Geo B, sup't, res 378 Pine

Wilner, Geo, shingle-packer, res 378 Pine

Wilson, Miss, dress-maker, s s Walnut, 2d w of Adams

Wilson, W B, proprietor of meat-market, s s Cherry, 6th e of Fox River House

Winegar, W H, res s s Crooks, 2d w of VanBuren

Winegar, Edward, sailor, 222 Main

Winnegar, Mrs Mary, boarding house, 222 Main

Winegard, Chas, clerk, 51 Cherry, bds cor Jefferson and Cherry

Windhauseer, M, shoemaker, bds n s Main, 3d e of VanBuren

Winslow, J R, res 156 Main

Winslow, R M, lumber merchant

Winslow, R S

Wisconsin Central R R Depot, foot of Adams

Wis Staats Zeitung, 27 and 29 Pine

Withem, Caleb, laborer, bds 378 Pine

Witmer, Mrs C, proprietor of saloon, 151 Washington

Winter, Thos, gunsmith, 147½ Washington, bds Bay City House

Whittiny, S N, physician, office and res e s Adams, 1st n of Doty

Woelz, Chris, merchant, store and res nw cor Main and Twelfth

WOELZ, C A, grocer, store and res w s Adams, 1st s of P O

Woelze, Frederick, harness maker, res nw cor Main and Twelfth

Woelze, Henry Sr, bds nw cor Main and Twelfth

Woelze, Henry, clerk, res nw cor Main and Twelfth

Wohlfriel, W, laborer, res s s Chicago 1st e of Eleventh

Wolf, H, butcher, bds ne cor Pine and Adams

Wolf, Mathias, proprietor, Bohemian House

Wolfan, Chas, laborer, res w s of Jackson, 1st s of Grignon

Wolfan, G, laborer, bds w s of Jackson, 1st s of Grignon
Wolfan, Mrs Jennie, wid, res nw cor of Quincy and Grignon
Wonser, Geo, teamster, res sw cor Doty and VanBuren
Wonser, Jasper, teamster, res sw cor Doty and VanBuren
Wood, E A, commission merchant, 74 Washington, res Ft Howard
Wood, Johnathan, res cor Elmore and Kelly, Ft Howard
Woodman, Andrew, laborer, res e s of Jefferson, 3d s of Mason
Woodruff, Miss Grace, clerk, 127 Washington, bds with H D Banister
Worthe, Frank, cook, bds Minnesota House
Wortz, Kittie, e s madison, 3d s of Crooks
Wright, C J, R R conductor, res n s Cherry 1st w of Quincy
Wright, Jessie F, lake sailor, res ne cor Cedar and Quincy
Wright, J T, pres't Green Bay Hide and Leather Co, bds 132 Main
Waynen, Albert, laborer, res s s Porlier, 1st w of Baird
Wyngaard, L, res s s Cherry, 1st e of Webster
WYNGAARD, M V D, flour and feed, n s of Main, 2d e of Beaumont House, res se cor Cherry and Webster
Wynhove, Herman, blacksmith, bds se cor Jefferson and Mason
Wyrz, J K T, res and saloon 128 Crooks
Wyers, Jacob, cooper, bds U S Hotel

Y

Yagadzeinski, Frank, furnaceman, res se cor Crooks and Twelfth
Yahn, M, tailor, res 263 Crooks
Yanda, Hannah, 84 Main st
YANDA, JOS, res and saloon 84 Main
Yaler, Wm, tanner, res n s Doty, 3d e of Twelfth
Yorke, Thos, liveryman, e end of Walnut st bridge, bds 2d e of bridge
Yongkind, Gabriel, laborer, res e s Adams, 4th s of Cass
Young, Andrew, res w s Quincy, 2d s of Pine
Young, C G, travelling salesman, res 140 Jefferson
Young, H, sailor, bds at Minnesota House
Young, P, bds e s Monroe, 1st n of Stuart
Young, John, res Main st, nr East River
Young, Kate, 96 Main
Young, S, car-smith, res n s Cass, 1st e of Adams
Younger, John, P, saloon, 141 Washington, res e s Monroe, 1st n of Stuart
Yuch, Chas, proprietor cigar store, bds Bay City House

Z

Zaepernick, C, tinner, res sw cor Quincy and Cedar
Zehrke, A F, policeman, res w s Jackson, 2d n of Stuart
Zephcrin, A J, bar tender, 43 Pine, res cor Harvey and
    Jackson
Ziegenspeck, A, tanner, bds n s Main, 3d w of Twelfth
Zinn, Wm, shoemaker, res w s Clay, 2d s of Cedar
Ziotkowski, M, carpenter, res s s Walnut, 2d e of Eleventh
Zottman, Jos, carpenter, res 39 Pine

Real Estate Office

OF

M. P. LINDSLEY,

ESTABLISHED 1857.

Lands & City Lots

BOUGHT AND SOLD.

LOANS NEGOTIATED,

MONEY INVESTED,

TAXES PAID &c.

GREEN BAY, WISCONSIN.

DIRECTORY OF PRINCIPAL BUSI-NESS HOUSES OF GREEN BAY.

ARCHITECTS

J McDonnuell, office 2d story 47 Pine
D M Harteau, office 2d story Shaylor block

ATTORNEYS

Bailey, W C, office over 1st National Bank (See adv)
Billings & Huntington, office cor Pine and Adams
Hastings & Green, office cor Pine and Adams
Hudd & Wigman, cor Pine and Washington (See adv)
Martin, M L, 142 Washington
Matile, G E, 109 Washington
Neville, Tracy & Neville, cor Pine and Washington (See adv)
Vroman & Sale, office 142 Washington st
Warren, O M, over 1st National Bank

BANKS

First National Bank, w s of Washington   (See adv)
Kellogg National Bank, 132 Washington   (See adv)
National Bank of Commerce, cor Washington and Pine

BARBER

J B Dufresne, cor Pine and Adams

CIGAR DEALERS

L H Dunlap, cor Pine and Adams
Fred Glahn, s s Pine bet Washington and Adams

CLOTHIERS

J Gotto, under Beaumont House
W Hoffman, No 105 Washington
Mueller & Hollmann, No 103 Washington

COMMISSION MERCHANTS

J V Stevens & Co, 74 Washington

CROCKERY

J Beth, 81 Washington
A Weise & Son, 93 Washington

DENTISTS
W C Corey, 140 Washington
A H Ellsworth, 123 Washington

DRY GOODS
D Butler & Son, 91 Washington
J Gotto, under Beaumont House
Holmes & Harteau, No 118 Washington
Skeels & Best, No 127 Washington

DYER
J Buscher, w s Washington bet Doty and Crooks

FLOUR AND FEED
Lamarre & Co, 78 Washington
Langton & Co, 106 Washington
Lefebvre & Wyngaard, n s Main, 2d e of Beaumont

FURNITURE
A Burkart, s s Main, 3d w of Jefferson

GROCERS
C Ahrberg, 154 Washington
Day, Koch & Co, (wholesale,) 92 Washington
E A Engels, cor Main and Jefferson
Joannes Bros, 120 Washington
Pinto & Co, 110 Washington
C A Woelz, w s Adams, 1st s of P O

HOTELS
Adams House, w s Adams, 1st n of Cherry
Beaumont House, cor Main and Washington
East River House, nr East River on Main
St Louis House, s s Main, 3d e of Adams
Waterloo House, n s Main, bet Adams and Jefferson

INSURANCE
E K Ansorge, 103 Washington
M V B Benson, over 1st National Bank
Ellis & Beards, cor Pine and Adams
Kimball & Libbey, 122 Washington
Williams & Warren, Shaylor Block, cor Pine and Adams

JEWELERS
E L Hall, 95 Washington
A Michaal, 29 Pine st
H J Ott & Co, 134 Washington

LAUNDRY
John St Dennis, w s Washington, 3d s of Crooks

LIQUOR DEALERS
Lawrence & Co, 136 Washington
A Smith, 109 Washington

LIVERY
L H Harriman, e s Jefferson, 2d s of 1st National Hotel
M E Roberts, n s of Walnut, 1st e of bridge

MACHINIST
J F Bertles, 179 Washington

MILLINERY
Mrs T McFayden, 116 Washington

MEAT MARKET
F Hagemeister. e s Adams, bet Main and Pine

MUSIC TEACHER
F Raisky, s s Main, 4th e of Adams

NOTARY
O J B Brice, cor Main and Adams

PAINTERS
T B Catlin, 96 Washington
F Criklair, 189 and 191 Adams
F M Lampson, 52 Walnut

PHOTOGRAPHER
W J Snelflohn 148 Washington

PHYSICIANS
D C Ayers, 149 Washington
B C Brett, office Fox' Block
D C L Fortier, 94 Washington
G A Lamb, 160 Washington
Pearce & Olmsted, s s Cherry bet Washington and Adams

H Schmidt, cor Adams and Cherry

PUBLISHERS

Green Bay Advocate, s s Pine, bet Washington and Adams
State Gazette, n s Pine, bet Washington and Adams
Wis Staats Zeitung, 27 and 29 Pine

REAL ESTATE

A Guesnier, 95 Washington
M P Lindsley, cor Pine and Adams
X Martin, 81 Washington

RESTAURANT

Williams & Garner, n s Pine, bet Adams and Washington
Herschede, Mrs E, s s Pine bet Adams and Washington

SALOONS

Home Saloon, No 115 Washington
Juenger, J P, proprietor saloon, 141 Washington
National Saloon, 97 Washington
C Pfotenhauer, proprietor saloon, cor Main and Adams
M E Roberts, proprietor saloon, n s Walnut, 2d e of Bridge
J Yanda, proprietor saloon 84 Main

STAVE DEALERS

H & J Dougherty, office Shaylor Block

UPHOLSTER

W H Marvin, 98 Washington

LAWRENCE UNIVERSITY, APPLETON, WISCONSIN

THE

City of Fort Howard,

WISCONSIN.

The history of Green Bay is necessarily, to a very great extent, the history of Fort Howard. Their settlement was simultaneous, and to all intents and purposes they always have been and always will be one city. Separated only by the Fox river they are united by Bridge and Ferry so completely that access from one to the other is at all times easy.

The Depots of the Chicago and Northwestern and the Green Bay and Minnesota Railroad lines are situated here. The trade of the place has thereby been much stimulated, and the population increased so rapidly, that it was thought best in furtherance of its prosperity, that a seperate city charter should be obtained, and in 1872 Fort Howard became a chartered city. Whether the two places shall always remain under different organizations or not is immaterial. In the eyes of the country at large they will always be considered as one. The population of Fort Howard is now about one-half that of Green Bay, and is rapidly increasing. The buildings of the old Fort which gave its name to the city, and for many years were objects of curiosity to the tourists have now disappeared, and the name of the city alone remains to perpetuate their memory.

The history of Fort Howard would not be at all complete with
out a description of the warehouse, docks and elevator of Messrs.
Elmore & Kelley, to whose enterprise very much of the prosperity
of Green Bay and Fort Howard is due.   The elevator is a most
substnatial structure,costing $80,000. and is 60x128 feet in size and
100 feet high.   It has a capacity of 25,000 bushels of wheat, ·
and can elevate 30,000 bushels of wheat per hour.   The largest
propellors find plenty of water beside it, and the railroad track
runs up to it.   The docks of Messrs Elmore & Kelley are 800 ft.
long, and a good depth of water is obtained for the entire length,
while the rail road track runs beside it, making it one of the most
convenient and extensive docks in the State.   A line of first class
propellors runs between these docks and Buffalo, leaving Fort
Howard twice each week.

    Another of the important enterprises of Fort Howard, and sec-
ond to none in adding to the growth of the city, is the Monitor
Iron Works, employing one hundred workmen, and turning out
such work as will but add to its daily growing reputation.

    We must not fail in this connection to speak of the Ft. Howard
boiler shops, where the style of workmanship is fully up to
the necessaries of the case, that is, to make secure, what is so
deadly in its results when of bad material or of poor workmanship.
These gentlemen can be relied upon in both these respects.

    The manufacturing establishment of C. Schwarz & Co. is also
entitled to more than a passing notice.   The employment it funi-
shes to the many who are engaged in its operation add to the material welfare of the city, while the gentlemanly proprietors justly
deserve the liberal patronage they receive.   All kinds of work
done in their line is performed by them in a neat and durable
manner, and speaks in glowing terms of their efficiency in their
line of business.

    The firm of J. P. Laird & Co. have done much also in improv-
ing the southern portion of the city.   Their mills for the manufacture of shingles, part of which are located here, give employment to many, while their manner of doing business is such as to
win them hosts of friends.

ST. ANDREWS SOCIETY OF GREEN BAY.

Prompted by a sense of duty and filial affection for their countrymen, a few of the patriotic sons of Auld Scotland met and re-
solved, in the fall of 1867, to form and organize a society of
Scotchmen, and further agreed that it should be named the " St.
Andrews Society of Green Bay." A Constitution was according-
ly framed and adopted by a duly organized body, and officers also
duly elected to hold office for one year, and perform their respective duties imposed upon them as prescribed in their constitution;
the officers to consist of President, 1st and 2d Vice Presidents,
Treasurer, Secretary, Corresponding Secretary, Chaplain, Physician, and a Board of Managers to look after the interest of subjects
that were entitled to the aid and counsel of said society, condit-
ioned in the constitution, and to report from time to time their
proceedings at the quarterly or yearly meetings in accordance
with their code of By-Laws. Said conditions empowered said
board to aid and counsel all Scotchmen, wives, sons and daughters
of Scotchmen, that might arrive on this great continent from other
shores seeking homes and employment, but more especially in this
section of country, to the relief necessary, whatever their circum-
stances might be, and in view of the foregoing facts, about 30 of
his most loyal sons rallied around the standard of their newly born
existence as a society, and pledged themselves in good faith to
each other by ascribing their respective names, and contributing
of their means to the Constitution, and to the charitable principles
therein involved.

In the fall of 1873 the society held its 6th anniversary, and in
honor due to it it has enjoyed through these years of unusual trial
very refreshing seasons of unalloyed joy in the quarterly and more
particularly in the yearly reunion of its members and friends, which
is one of the leading features in the organization, where they may
have time and opportunity to meet together at least once in the
year to to encourage, to sympathise, and to cultivate and extend to
each other that brotherly love so necessary (in this world and in
the world to come) in the protection and fostering of all true hap-
piness. And although at periods during the lapse of time its

members have been greatly augmented by accessions that it rejoic-
ed over, and diminished by removals and deaths that it mourned
over, nevertheless the standing of its membership has been re-
markably uniform and tranquil, and at the present day it has on
its roll about 40 good and faithful members, and would here extend a cordial invitation to all their loyal and sympathizing
countrymen to come forward and join in in their ranks, and co-
operate with them in their good work of mercy.   Relief has been
extended to the needy in several instances, with humility and
fullness of heart from donor and receiver, aid and counsel to
to others in varied forms, which was invariably received with
gratitude, and in every instance where needed assistance or char-
ity has come under the observation of the Managers, or even the
members, they have come to the rescue; and may God speed the
designs and philanthropic principals of this society.

   The present Secretary, William Hood, was chosen its first
President, and the present Mayor of the City of Fort Howard,
Hon. David Burns, is its present President.

   Intermediate President's names as follows:

James Ritchie, De Pere.

Andrew Reid,   "

Robt. Mailer,   "   (two terms.)

James Miller,   "

N. B. The Rev. Alex. Hamilton, Baptist minister, was chosen
Chaplain of the society.   He resided in Fort Howard at the time
of its origin.   He still holds the honorable office although he now
resides in Waukau, Wisconsin.

Fort Howard, Wis. August 22d, 1874.

MORAVIAN CHURCH.

   Located on corner of Fourth Street and Fifth Avenue.

   Services Sunday 10:30 A. M. and 2:30 P. M.   Sunday School
3:30 P. M.

   Rev. A. M. Iverson, Pastor.   Residence south-east corner
Fourth Street and Fifth Avenue.

This society was organized Sept. 21st, 1866, by the present
pastor, with but seven communicants and about twenty non-communicants. Its services were at first held in a school building,
where this infant congregation was wont to assemble, In a short
time they had the misfortune to loose the faithful services of their
worthy pastor, and were more or less scattered until he was again
induced to return to his former home and the charge of that flock
of which he was the moving spirit in its organization. Gladly was
his advent among them received, and with redoubled energy and
faith, they set about the work of calling together again the wand-
ering portion of their fold.   And how well they labored is seen
when we take into consideration the fact that at the expiration of
only a few years they were enabled to dedicate their own beautiful little church, entirely free from incumbrance, an honor to
themselves and a fitting tribute of devotion to their Master. Since
that time their growth has been steady and permanent, and they
now have a membership of forty-nine communicants and twenty
non-communicants, with a property valued at $5,000.

NORWEGIAN EVANGELICAL LUTHERAN CHURCH.

Located on Broadway.
Services Sunday at 10:30 A. M. and 7:30 P. M.
Rev. T. H. Dahl, Pastor.
The society was organized January 6th, 1867, with a membership of thirty-seven communicants, under the pastoral care of
Rev. S. M. Kregnaes, who continued his services until July of
the same year. The Rev. J. Olsen then assumed the duties of
pastorate, and the following month commenced the erection of a
church edifice, which was completed in the same year. In Jan.
1873, the present pastor accepted the pastorate, and in the fall of
the same year commenced the enlargement of the church, and
added thereto a spire, all of which was completed in May of 1874.
The whole cost of structure being now about $3,500.

The prosperity of the society since its organization has been very flattering, and speaks well for those in charge as also the society. Organized with a membership, as previously stated, of but thirty-six, it has now increased to one hundred and seventy, and is in a fair way to increase its membership.

METHODIST EPISCOPAL CHURCH.

Located on north-east corner Broadway and Hubbard Streets. Services Sunday 10:30 A. M. and 7:30 P. M.

Rev. Mathew Evans, Pastor. Residence west side of Cedar, between Hubbard and Dousman Streets.

This society was organized October 16th, 1869, with thirty-five members, and has increased in growth and prosperity until it now numbers eighty members, and has a property valued at about $2,200.

CONGREGATIONAL CHURCH.

Located on south west corner Fourth Avenue and Third Streets.

Services Sunday 10:30 A. M. and 7:30 P. M.

D. C. Curtis, Pastor.

The Congregational Church in Fort Howard was organized January 6th, 1855, with membership of seven. The first minister was Rev. Charles W. Monroe, who served the church from its origen to May 1st, 1856, 16 months Under his supervision a house of worship was built. The second minister was J. T .Marsh, who commencing labor Sept. 1st 1857, served one year. From Sept. 1855 to Nov. 1863 all public services were suspended. They were then resumed under the ministry of the present acting pastor Rev. D. C. Curtis, the church consisting of ten members. The whole number which has been added to the church is ninety. Present membership sixty-one.

BAPTIST CHURCH.

The Baptist Church in Fort Howard is situated near the North East corner of Chestnut and Main Streets. The Pastor is Rev. F. S. Witter, whose residence is at the parsonage North of and adjoining the church.

The Sabbath morning service is at 10:30 o'clock, to which strangers are most cordially invited. The evening service is at 7 P. M. The Sabbath School is at 12 M., the Superintendent of which is Mr. O. Gray. Prayer meeting Wednesday-eve in the session room of the church at 7:30 P. M. Young Folks' devotional meeting Thursday-eve at the same hour and place.

The church was organized in Green Bay in September. 1851. It began with seven members and now has one hundred and seven. It was afterward transplanted to the western shore of the River in Fort Howard. Under the pastorate of Rev. S. Adams the first church edifice was built. The present pastor, Rev. F. S· Witter, waa called from Iowa, and preached his first sermon in Fort Howard October 13th, 1872. He was educated in the state of New York for the law, and was ordained in 1871. One of the most remarkable revivals that ever visited a City occurred under his pastorate. The pastor baptized ten from his Bible class of young men and women. The whole City was stirred, and the membership of his church more than doubled in nine weeks. Under his pastotate the present new and elegant church edifice, the finest in the City, and one of the best in the State, was built, The architect is J. McDonnell of Green Bay. The style is decorated Gothic. It is 34x58, chancel 10x13, pastor's library and study each 9x14, session room 43x12. The main spire on the corner is 115 high. The whole church is furnished with stained windows, and of beautiful octagon glass made by Misch & Bro., 217 East Water street, Chicago. Clark & Brown of Appleton, Wis., builders. The stranger can find a free seat in this elegant House of Worship and a hospitable reception.

POST OFFICE

The Post Office is under the management of J. Taylor, with J. H. Taylor assistant.

The amount of business transacted at this office may be seen at a glance, by examining the following:
Number of letters passed through the office per month, about 2,000.
Money orders, issued and received $2,800.
Registered packages, 1,800.
The boxes, about 400 in number, are conveniently arranged, and no pains are spared on the part of P. M. and assistant to accomodate the public. Office hours, 6:30 A. M. to 7:30 P. M. Sunday 9 to 10 A. M.

FIRE DEPARTMENT.

The Fire Department of Fort Howard, although limited in extent, is an important auxiliary in protection of property against the fire fiend. The engine is of the Button & Son manufacture, of third class, and thus far has proved itself a first class Engine. It is a matter of credit to the different Fire companies of Green Bay and Fort Howard, that they mutually assist each other and in this manner increase the efficiency of each.

Such good feeling and unity of purpose cannot but prove pleasant to their members, as also beneficial to the Cities.

The water supply has heretofore been the Fox River, but drains are now being laid from it to supply reservoirs in different parts of the city, which cannot but prove valuable in time of need.

OFFICERS AND COMMITTEES.

CITY OFFICERS.

David Burns, *Mayor*; Joel S Fisk, *Treasurer*; James Delaney, *Assessor*; D. Hunt, *Clerk*; Abm. Lucas, *Marshal*; D. Hunt, *Police Justice*; W. C. Bailey, *City Attorney*; Rob't. Chappell, *Sup't. of Schools.*

MEMBERS OF COMMON COUNCIL.

First Ward—A. Gray, G. Richardson, John Salvo.
Second Ward—C. Schwarz, N. C. Foster, Julius S. Fisk.
Third Ward—B. J. Smith, S. Anderson, H. Ehle.
Regular meetings of the council—First Monday in each month.

STANDING COMMITTEES.

Finance—Richardson, Foster and Anderson.
Accounts—Schwarz, Gray and Ehle.
Ordinances—Fisk, Salvo and Smith.
Fire Department—Smith, Foster and Richardson.
Printing—Schwarz, Smith and Anderson.
Streets and Bridges—Fisk, Smith and Salvo.
Taverns and Groceries—Gray, Fisk and Ehle.
Public Grounds—Foster, Salvo, and Anderson.

SUPERVISORS.

C. C. Lovett, First Ward; U. H. Peak, Second Ward; L. Howland, Third Ward.

WARD BOUNDARIES.

The First Ward is bounded on the north by city limits, east by Fox River, south by north line of private claim No. 1, and west by city limits.

The Second Ward is bounded on the north by north line of private claim No. 1, on the east by Fox River, on the south by north line of private claim No. 2, and on the west by city limits.

The Third Ward is bounded on the north, by north line of private claim No. 2, east by Fox River, south by city limits, and west by city limits.

STREET DIRECTORY.

Fox River on the east of city, is taken as a guide for streets running north and south, and all streets are numbered from it. Main street being that upon which is located the Fox River bridge, is taken as a guide for the streets paralled with it, and they are numbered north and south from it.

Baird street, 1st south of Main, and extends from River west to Willow.

Broadway street, 3d west of River, and extends north and south the length of First and Second Ward.

Bond street, 5th north of Main, and extends from Broadway west to city limits.

Cedar street, 5th west of River, and extends north from the slough to city limits.

Chestnut street, 4th west of River, and extends from slough, north to city limits.

Cherry street, 5th west of River, and extends north from the slough to city limits.

Cornell street, 7th north of Main, and extends west from Broadway to city limits.

Dousman street, 2d north of Main, and extends west from River to city limits.

Dennis street, 8th north of Main, and extends west from Broadway to city limits.

Elmore street, 4th north of Main, and extends west from Broadway to city limits.

Eighth Avenue, 8th west of River, and extends south from 2d slough bridge to Ninth st.

Eighth street, 8th south of slough, and extends west from 2d Avenue to the slough.

Fourth Avenue, 4th west of River, and extends south from Laird & Co's. Mill to Ninth st.

Fourth street, 4th south of slough, and extends east and west from Third to 5th Avenue.

Fifth Avenue, 5th west of River, and extends south from 1st slough to Ninth st.

Fifth street, 5th south of slough, and extends west from C. & N. W. R'y. to the Oneida road.

First street, 1st south of slough, and extends west from Third
Avenue to Oneida road.

Hubbard street, 1st north of Main, and extends west from
River to Willow st.

John street, 2d south of Main, and extends west from River
to Chestnut st.

Kellogg street, 3d north of Main, and extends west from
Broadway to city limits.

Main street, extends west from Fox River bridge to city
limits.

Mather street, 6th north of Main, and extends west from
Broadway to city limits.

Ninth Avenue, 9th west of River, and extends south from 1st
slough to 9th st.

Ninth street, 9th south of 1st slough, and extends west from
Second Avenue to 2d slough.

Pearl street, 2d west of River, and extends north from John
st to C. & N. W. R'y. Co's. land

Second Avenue, 2d west of River, and extends south from
2d slough bridge to Ninth st.

Second street, 2d south of slough, and extends from C. & N.
W. R'y. to the Oneida road.

Sixth Avenue, 6th west of River, and extends south from 1st
slough to Ninth st.

Seventh Avenue, 7th west of River, and extends south from
1st slough to 9th st.

Seventh street, 7th south of slough, and extends west fr   1
River to 2d slough.

Third Avenue, 3d w of River, and extends south fro·
slough bridge to 9th st.

Third street, 3d south of slough, and extends west fr ·
N. W. R'y. to Oneida road.

Waite street, 1st w of River, and extends north fro··
Hubbard st.

Willow street, 7th west of River, and extends ·
slough to city limits.

GREEN BAY
AND
Minnesota
((RAILROAD,))
AND CONNECTIONS.

Rand, McNally & Co., Map Eng'rs, Chicago.

FORT HOWARD

⮘ CITY ⮚

DIRECTORY.

1874-5.

A

Acker, Henry P, machinist, r 61 Main

Acker, H P, machinist Monitor Iron Works, res e s of Broadway 2d s of Second st

Ackerman, George, pattern maker Monitor Iron Works, res Green Bay

Adams, Almira Miss, servant 25 Kellogg, between Chestnut and Broadway

Adolf —, laborer 255 Dousman, 9th w Willom

Albert, J, teamster, res n s Fourth st, 2d e Fifth Avenue

Alland, Moses, gardner, res Main, w Willow

Allan, Chas, boiler maker, res n s Dousman, 5th w Willow

Allen, Chas, boiler maker, res n s Dousman, 5th e of Villa

Allen, Jas, carpenter G B & M R R, res w s of Broadway, 3d n

Allen, Frank, fireman G B & M R R, res w s of Broadway, 3d n of Third

Allen, J B, carpenter, res w s of Broadway, 3d n of Third st
Allen, C J, boiler maker, bds Fort Howard House
Allen, J B, locomotive engineer, bds s s Mather, 2d w Cherry
Allen, Hamilton, carpenter, res w s of Broadway, 3d n of Third
 street
Alling, E L, carpenter, res e s Sixth Avenue, 1st s of G B & M
 R R
Alling, L K. tin-smith, res n e cor Seventh Avenue and First st
Alling, H E, carpenter, res e s Sixth Avenue, 1st s of G B & M
 R R
Amenson, Ole, laborer, res s s Fourth st, next to Moravian
 Church
Anderson, Andrew, laborer, res near Chestnut s of Baird
Anderson, A G, laborer, res e s Broadway, 2d n Fifth
Anderson, M, sailor, bds cor Fifth Avenue and First
Anderson, J, laborer, bds ne cor Fifth Avenue and First st
Anderson, H, laborer, res cor Fifth Avenue and First st
Anderson, T, Prop grocery store, res sw cor Broadway and
 Third
Anderson, S. laborer, res ne cor Fourth Avenue and Fifth
Andersen, T, (Andersen & Ellingsen) grocer, w s of Broadway,
 2d n of Third
Anderson, U, baker, w s of Broadway, 2d s of Second
Anderson, Andrew, laborer, res w s Broadway, 4th s Ninth
Anderson, Annie, servant, bds e s Fourth Avenue, 2d n Eighth
Anderson, Tone, (L Nelson & Co) res s s Main, 2d w Broad-
 way
Andersen, Iver, res e s Broadway, 2d s of Main
Anderson, Henry, laborer, res e s Fourth Avenue, 2 n of Eighth
Anderson, Albert, clerk Jencks & Clinton, res e s Broadway, bet
 Main and Bond
Anderson, C, sailor, res s s Third, w Broadway
Anderson, S, ship-builder, res ne cor Fourth st and Fifth Avenue
Anderson, Stancy, sewing girl, res ne cor Fifth Avenue and Fifth
Anderson, P. ship-carpenter, res ne cor Fifth Avenue and First
Anderson, H, boot and shoe maker, w s of Pearl 4th n of Main.
 res same
Anderson, Fred, carpenter. res near Chestnut s of Baird
Anderson, Tim, section man, res e s Cherry, 1st s Main
Anderson, A, ship-carpenter, bds s s Fourth st 1st w Broadway
Andersen, Charles A, res w s Broadway, bet Hubbard and Main
Anderson, N, tailor, res nw cor Fifth Avenue and Third
Anderson, K. painter, res e s Sixth Avenue. 2d s of Third
Archibald, John, captain yacht. res s s Hubbard 1st e of Cedar
Armstrong, W. caulker, res w s Fifth Avenue, 1st s G B & M
 R R

Arnold, Gilbert C, lumberman, res s s Hubbard, 1st e Willow
Artel, Thomas, laborer, res e s Cherry, 2d s Hubbard
Atkinson, Stephen, cattle broker, res sw cor Dousman and Willow
Atkinson, Henry, cattle broker, res sw cor Dousman and Willow
Atkinson, Kate, dressmaker and milliner, res sw cor Dousman and Willow
Aul, E I, machinist, res John st

B

Bahn, Michael, laborer, res s s Bond, w Cedar
Bailey, Henry, wood turner, res ne cor Chestnut and Baird
Bailey, Thomas J, wood turner, res e s Chestnut, bet Main and Baird
Baker, Carry, servant, nw cor Cherry and Baird
Baker, Flora, servant, e s of Broadway, 4th s of Second st
Baker, J H, teamster, res w s Sixth Avenue, 1st s of First st
Bakken, S, tailor, res n s Fourth st, 2d w Broadway
Barkley, Rob't, operator, res n s Kellogg, bet Chestnut and Broadway
Barlment, Geo, horse dealer, res Mather, w Willow
Bartran, W H, physician, res w s Chestnut, 2d n Main
Bauerfend, E, carpenter, C Schwarz & Co, res Green Bay
Bay Brewery, F Blesch, proprietor, w s of Pearl, n of Main
Becker, A, photograph artist, bds s s Fifth st, 1st w C & N W R R
Becker, Mrs Helda, res s s Fifth st, 1st w C & N W R R
Becker, Gotleib, laborer, bds at Wis Hotel
Becket, W, shoemaker, res n s Third st, 2d e Fourth Avenue
Belanger, Joseph, laborer, res Mather, w Willow
Belanger, N, saloon and billard room, Whitney House, nw cor Main and Broadway, bds Whitney House
Bell, Thomas, moulder, Monitor Works, res n s Chestnut, bet Main and Baird
Bell, William, pattern maker, res w s Chestnut, 2d s Main
Bellew, Matthias, blacksmith, res n s Hubbard, nr Pearl
Bender, Paul, hardware, n s of Main, 4th e of Broadway, res Pearl st
Bentler, Julius, carpenter, C Schwarz & Co, res e s Broadway, bet Baird and John
Bently, W H, cooper, e s Broadway, bet Baird and ——, bds Whitney House
Bentley, G, carpenter, res sw cor Seventh Avenue, and First
Benningham, Anna Mrs, grocery and provision, sw cor Hubbard and Cherry, res same

J. P. LAIRD & CO.,

MANUFACTURERS OF AND DEALERS IN

LUMBER,

SHINGLES.

LATH & PICKETS.

OFFICE AND MILLS, THIRD WARD,

FORT HOWARD, WIS.

Berendson, A G, proprietor of meat market, w s of Broad-
way, 4th n of Third st
Berghman, Julius, mason and builder, res n s Second st, 2d e
of Fifth Avenue
Bergner, Louis, carpenter, C Schwarz & Co, res Clark
Bersenger, P. ship-carpenter, res se cor Avenue, and Third st
Bersenger, Geo. laborer, bds ne cor Fifth Avenue and Third
Bersenger, N, gardener, res ne cor Fifth Avenue and Third st
Bertanel, William H Dr, School Board Ft Howard
Biske, Wm, carpenter, C Schwarz & Co, res w s Broadway,
bet Baird and John
Bitter, Henry, carpet weaver, res w s Broadway, 3d s Eighth
Black, R J, foreman in G B & M y'd, res ne cor Second st
and Ninth Avenue
Blair, A M, reporter, bds Ft Howard House
Blair, E, laborer, bds e s Fifth Avenue, 3d s Ninth st
Blair, Henry, laborer, res e s Fifth Avenue, 3d s Ninth st
Blair, J, laborer, bds e s Fifth Avenue, 3d s Ninth st
Blesch, Miss Sophia, music teacher, res at Bay Brewery
Blesch, Miss Clara, school teacher, res at Bay Brewery
Blesch, F, proprietor Bay Brewery, res at Brewery
Blichfeldt, J A, proprietor of Scand'n Hotel, Pearl st
Blichfeldt, Mrs J, wid, res next n of Scand'n House
Blichfeld, Frank, clerk for Hall & Burns, res w s of Pear
next n of Scand'n House
Blodgett, J, laborer, res se cor Ninth st and Fourth Avenue
Boland, Edward, clerk, res n s Kellogg, 2d e Cherry .
Borkenhagen, B, res s s Second st, bet Fifth & Sixth Avenue
Boutain, Joseph, fish packer, M F Kalmbach, res n s Main.
1st w bridge
Bowen, C W, car repairer, res e s Eighth Avenue, 3d n
Second st
Bradner, Chas C, book-keeper, M F Kalmbach, bds w
Cherry, 2d n Dousman
Brady, Jas, bds Broadway House
Brahy, N, blacksmith, Howard Foundry
Braigger, W, tin-smith, res nw cor Fourth Avenue & Seco:
Brannan, James, carpenter, res w s Cedar, 4th n Main
Brehme, Aug, wagon maker, E Brehme, res cor Chesti
and Baird
Brehme, E, wagon maker and blacksmith, w s Broadway,
s Main, res same
Brehme, Anton, boiler maker, res n s Pearl, 2d n John
Brehme, Charles, carpenter, res w s Pearl, 2d n John
Brehme, Aug, clerk, Wm Gray, res w s Broadway, 3d s \'
Brewer, Ben, R R fireman, bds Corniucopia House

FISH DEPOT

M. F. KALMBACH,

WHOLESALE & RETAIL DEALER IN ALL KINDS OF

FRESH AND SALT

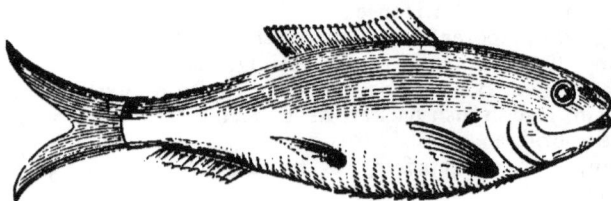

LAKE SUPERIOR TROUT A SPECIALTY.

DEPOT WEST END OF MAIN STREET BRIDGE.

FORT HOWARD, WISCONSIN.

Brewick, P, shoemaker, res sw cor Fourth Avenue & Second
Brickner, H, carpenter, res w s Fifth Avenue, head Fourth
Broadway House, C McGinnis, proprietor, w s Broadway, bet Hubbard and Dousman
Broker, C J, shoemaker, s s Hubbard, bet Broadway & Pearl
Brown, Jonas G, carpenter, res s s Hubbard, 2d e Cedar
Bromley, VanBuren, lawyer, (G B,) res sw cor Main & Cedar
Brooks, J, laborer, res sw cor Seventh Avenue and Fifth st
Brown, John, laborer, res e s Eighth Avenue, opp park
Brownfield, John, bds Broadway House
Brsner, J, laborer, res sw cor Fourth Avenue and Ninth st
BRUCE, W G, (W G Bruce & Co,) res sw Hubbard & Cedar
BRUCE, W H, groceries, w s Broadway, 2d n Whitney House, res 104 Hubbard
Brunette, David, pensioner, res Main. w Willow
Brunette, John, farmer, res w s Broadway, bet Tenth and Eleventh sts
Brillie, Jas, res w s Broadway, opp Moravian Church
Burns, D, proprietor Ft Howard boiler works, e s Pearl, 2d s Main
Burmeister, Henry, merchant tailor, e s Pearl, 2d n of Main
Burk, Richard, eng C & N W R R, bds Sherman House
Burns, David, Sec'y and Treas, Monitor Iron Works Co, res sw cor Hubbard and Chestnut
Burns, Thos Jr, clerk, w s of Pearl, 9th n of Main
Burns, T H, (Hall & Burns,) hardware, w s of Broadway, 3d n of Main, res Broadway
Burns, Wm, laborer, bds Cornuicopia House
Burns, Tho, hardware, res e s Broadway, 2d w Baird
Burns Thos, proprietor saloon & grocery, res w s Pearl, 9th n of Main
Burstem, R, machinist, w s Chestnut, 3d s Baird
Burstem, Thos, carpenter, res e s Chestnut, 2d s Baird
Burton, Stephen, carpenter, res Mather and Willow
Bygdall, G, laborer, res e s Seventh Avenue, 3d s of Third st

C

Cable, Emil, carpenter, res sw cor Seventh Avenue & Third st
Cady, L, servant, res e s Sixth Aavenue, 1st s of G B & M R R
Calhul, Bridget, sev't, sw cor Chestnut and Hubbard
Calkins, Charles B, (Foster & Calkins,) res w s Cedar, 4th n Main
Callaghan, James, dry goods and groceries, w s Broadway, 1st n Hubbard
Camm, C M Mrs, physician, res sw cor Cedar and Dousman

23

CAMM, THOS M, groceries boots and shoes and crockery, se cor Main and Broadway, res cor Main and Chestnut

Camm Geo, night-watch, res sw cor Cedar and Dousman

Camm, T M, shoemaker, res sw cor Cedar and Dousman

Camp, Daniel, merchant, res w s Broadway, nw cor Bond and Broadway

Cannon, E A, mail ag't, res e s Cedar, 3d n Dousman

John, Carle, farmer, res e s broadway, 1st n city limits

Carter, Eugene, broom-maker, res Mather, w Willow

Carter, W A, printer Monitor office, bds Cherry, bet Main and Hubbard

Casey, Thos, mason, res e s Pearl, 4th s Main

Casey, Maggie, sev't, Whitney House

Casperson, Mathias, sailor, res n w cor Broadway and Third st

Chappell, Rob't, city sup't schools, res Main, w Willow

Christ, Andrew, teamster, C Schwarz & Co, res e s Broadway, bet Baird and John

Christenson, Andrew, teamster, res w s Chestnut

Christiansen, Ole, laborer, bds w s Pearl, n Scand'n Hotel

Christensen, Peter, carpenter, bds at Union House

Christenson, Maria, sev't, w s Cherry, 2d s Main

Chlausen, Lars, laborer, res e s Broadway, bet Main and Baird

Christainson, A, laborer, res w s Seventh Avenue, 2d n school-house

Christainson, Andrew, laborer, res w s Fourth Avenue, 2d s Ninth st

Christianson, L C, laborer, res se cor Fifth Avenue & Second st

Churchill, J T H, farmer, res Mather, w Willow

Civink, J, laborer, res w s 4th Avenue, 2d s Eighth st

Clark, D, carpenter and joiner, res n s Third st, 2d e Fourth

Clark, Michael, proprietor Ft Howard saloon, w s Broadway, 2d n Second st

Clark, Miss Jennie, school teacher, res nw co Broadway and Second st

Clausen, L, laborer, C Schwarz & Co, res Broadway, bet Main and Baird

Cleary, Patrick, laborer, res s s Elmore, w Willow

Clementson, M, ship-carpenter, res e s Fifth Avenue, s of Moravian Church

Clernnan, J, saloon keeper, res Mather, w Willow

Clernnan, Alex, saloon keeper, res Mather, w Willow

Cline, Martin, engineer, res ne cor Baird and Willow

Cline, Thos, machinista, res ne cor Baird and Willow

Clinton, Dewitt C, (Jenks & Clinton,) bds Whitney House

Coan, Mary, servant, 28 Cedar

Cobb, A C, gas fitter, res e s Willow, bet Main and Baird

Codey, Dennis, res sw cor Broadway and Second st
Codey, Sohn, sawyer, res sw cor Broadway and Second st
Cody, J, works on C & N W R R, res e s Broadway, 2d s Third st
Colburn, D H Mrs, proprietor Home Laundry, e s Broadway, 4th s Dousman
Coleman, Mary, servant, sw cor Cedar and Main
Coll, John, laborer, res Mather, w Willow
Collins, Thos, porter, Cornucopia House
Colpin, F, machinist, Monitor Iron Works
Condon, E, laborer, res se cor Second st and Fourth Avenue
Congregational Church, sw cor Fourth Avn, and Third street
Conley, Vincent, boat-builder, res Fowles' ship yard
Connopy, Michael, laborer, w s Cedar, 5th n Main
Connor, Hugh, laborer, res e s Broadway bet Baird and ——
Conway, P H, laborer, res s s Bond bet Willow and Cherry
Conyah, Augusta, servant, Ft Howard House
Cooley, W H, baggage master, bds sw cor Seventh Avenue and Third st
Cornucopia House, w s Pearl, bet Main and Hubbard, J M Slater, proprietor
Corbett, M J, machinist, bds Ft Howard House
Cormick, Alex, laborer, n s Cedar, bet Elmore and Kellogg
Cornell, Hiram, stock ag't, res w s Broadway bet Bond and Mather
Cradame, L A, res Main, w Willow
Craney, C, engineer, C & N W R R, res n s Dousman, 2d w Willow
Crocker, Ephraim, sheriff of Brown Co, res w s Broadway, bet Main and Hubbard
Crocker, Frank E, res w s Broadway, bet Main & Hubbard
Culver, Gordon H, ticket ag't, C & N W R R, res w s Chestnut, bet Dousman and Hubbard
Culpin, Frantz, laborer, res s s Elmore, 3d w Willow
Cumming, H A, servant, ne cor Main and Chestnut
Currin, Mat, bds Broadway House
Curtis, Miss Hattie, school teacher, res nw cor Sixth Avenue and Third st
Curtis, Miss Julia, music teacher, res n w cor Sixth Avenue and Third st
Curtis, Mrs S B, wid, proprietor of boarding house, sw cor of Seventh Avenue and Third st
Curtis, D C, clergyman, res nw cor Sixth Avenue and Third st
Cusick, John, laborer, res s s Dousman, 3d w Willow

D

Dagen, C, engineer on G B & M R R, res, w s Fifth Avenue.
2d s Ninth

Daggett, C M, sawyer, res n s First st, 2d e of Seventh Avenue

Dahl, Theo H Rev, pastor Norwegian Lutheran Church, res
Chestnut, s of Bond

Danes, A B, clerk W G Bruce & Co, bds Whitney House

Darcey, Martin, bds at Cornucopia House

Davis, A D, teamster, res s s Dousman, 1st w Willow

Davidson, A. C. clerk in bank, bds n s Fifth st 2d w of Fourth
Avenue

Davidson, machinist C Schwarz & Co, res n s Fifth st, 2d w
Fourth Avenue

Davidson, Thos, carpenter C. Schwarz & Co, res Fifth st

DeGraet, Joseph, laborer, res s s Cedar bet Kellogg and Elmore

De Gracie, C, laborer, res n s Second st, 2d e Fourth Avenue

Deidricht, J, prop saloon, res e s Third Avenue, 2d s Ninth st

Dehon, E, machinist Monitor Works

Delaney, James, agent for ties C & N W R R, res n w cor Broadway aud Ninth st

Delaney, T, filer, res sw cor of Sixth Avenue and Second st

De La Porte, Fanny. dressmaker. bds ne cor Main aud Cedar

De La Porte, Minnette, res ne cor Main and Cedar

Dennessen, John, laborer, res s s Kellogg, bet Cedar and Cherry

Dean, Jas, dyer, res e s Pearl, 1st n Howard Foundry

Denney, Mich. brakesman C & N W R R, bds at Sherman
House

De Pere, Perie, laborer, res n s Chestnut, bet Kellogg and
Elmore

Doherty, T, laborer, res ne cor Fourth Avenue and Fourth st

Domandel, J. stone-mason, res n s Second s 1st e Fifth Avenue

Doran, John, laborer, res e s Willow, n Baird

Doty, Miss Emma, compositor, bds e s Cherry, bet Dousman and
Kellogg

Doty, Elisha, carpenter, bds n s Cherry, bet Dousman and
Cherry

Doty, Wesley, mason, res nw cor Kellogg and Cherry

Dousman House, se cor Dousman and Broadway, Anthony Mountain Propr

Doyen, Silas L, drugggist cor Main and Broadway, res w s Cherry
bet Dousman and Hubbard

Doyle, Mrs J, wid, res e s Ninth Avenue, 3d n Second st

Doyle, J, laborer, res e s Ninth Avenue, 2d n Second st

Doyle, James. laborer. res sw cor John and Broadway

Doyen. Silas L, druggist, res Chestnut, bet Dousman and Hubbard

Drion, Gustave, book peddler, res s s Elmore, w Willow
Driscoll, Alice, servant w s Chestnut 4th s Hubbard
Dugan, John, blacksmith G B & M R R, res e s Broadway. 2d s of Second st
Duhl, Rev F H, pastor Lutheran Church
Dukeek, Anna, servant se cor Willow and Hubbard
Duncan, Archie, machinist, res ne cor Main and Cherry
Duncan, J Jr, machinist Howard Foundry
DUNCAN, JOHN, (Taylor & Duncan) res ne cor Main and Hubbard
Duncan, Thomas, telegraph operator, res ne cor Main and Cherry
Dunlap, Gilbert L, carpenter, res w s Chesnut, 3d s Hubbard
Dunlap, Gil, res Main n of Willow
DUNLAP, LYMAN H, cigars wholesale, res n s Chestnut, 3d s Hubbard
Dworeihk, F, carpenter, res nw cor Sixth Avenue and Ninth st

E

Earl, Charles, bds sw cor Cherry and Mather
Ech, Anton, laborer, res w s Fourth Avenue 3d s Eighth Avenue
Ehle, Herman, carpenter, res w s Broadway, 2d s Third st
Ehensperger, Henry, machinist, res e s of Pearl, 2d s of Monitor Iron Works
Eismann, J G, res Maine w Willow
Elderkin, H R, physician, res ne cor Elm and Dousman
Eleson, H, ship-carpenter, res w s Third Avenue, 1st s Seventh street
Eliason, M, ship-capenter, res w s Third Avenue 2d s Seventh street
Ellingsen, G, (Anderson & Ellingsen) grocer w s of Broadway 2d n of Third
Ellingson, J, carpenter, res n s Fifth, 2d w Broadway
Elmore, Andrew E, capitalist, res w s Broadway 1st n Freight Depot
ELMORE, JAS. H commission merchant res n s Broadway. 1st n of Depot
Engelsen, Axel, laborer, res e s Broadway, 2d s Dousman
Engstram, Sophia, wid res w s Broadway, 1st s Fourth st
Enc, Michael, laborer, res 49 Cedar
Erickson, Andrew, laborer, bds w s Broadway, 4th s Third st
Erickson, A. works in mill, bds nw cor Fifth Avenue and First street
Erickson, J, laborer, res nw cor Fifth Avenue and First st
Erwin, Joseph, master mechanic, res e s Chestnut
Evans, Rev Mather, pastor M E Church, res e s Cedar 1st s of Hubbard

F

Fahey, Thomas, section master, res w s Chestnut 2d n Kellogg
Faireker. H, foundryman Taylor & Duncan
Farann, Richard, laborer, res n s Elmore w Willow
Farnsworth, Wm, res nw cor Broadway and Second st
Farell, T, Foreman G B & M Round House, bds ne cor Sixth
    Avenue and Third st
Faulkner, Jas, boot and shoe manufacturer e s Pearl 2d n of
    Main, res Broadway
Faulkner, W, moulder Howard Foundry
Felch W W, barber shop 2d story McCartney Block, res se cor
    Cherry and Elmore
Feldt, A, painter, bds at Union House
Felix, — market gardener, res n s Dousman 7th w Willow
Ferhein, Loenaul, laborer, bds s s Elmore bet Chestnut and
    Cherry
Fink, Dan C, foreman Monitor office, res nw cor Cherry and
    Elmore
Finnan, John, bds Broadway House
Firaiken, J. machinist Howard Foundry
Fischer, Frank, propr New London House, se cor Pearl
Fishe, S, blacksmith, res e s Seventh Avenue, 3d s of First st
Fisher, J, millwright, res ne cor of Broadway and Second st
Fisk, Henry, clerk Julius S Fisk, res w s Chestnut opposite Bap-
    tist Church
Fisk, Julius S, grocer ne cor Pearl and Main, r w s Chestnut op-
    posite Baptist Church
Fisk, William, planing mill, bds w s Broadway 4th s Baird
Fisk, Joel S, City Treasurer of Fort Howard, res e s Chestnut.
    2d n Baptist church
Fisk, Wm J, capitalist. res nw cor Main and Willow
Flanigan, Annie servant Cornucopia House
Flanigan, Ellen, servant Cornucopia House
Flatley, H, grocer w s of Pearl 2d n of Main, res Chestnut
Flatley, Mrs Patrick, wid, res e s Willow bet Main and Baird
Forest City House, w s of Pearl n of Main
Ford, Thos, laborer, bds Cornucopia House
Ford, James K, machinist and engineer, res sw cor Cherry and
    Mather
Fort Howard House, James Tiernan propr, sw cor Main and
    Pearl
Fort Howard engine No 1, w s Pearl bet Main and Baird, Peter
    Sheridan engineer, John Voight foreman
Fort Howard Monitor, 2d story McCartney block, David Mc-
    Cartney propr

Fort Howard Herald, C J Pratt propr, office n s of Maine 4th e
of Broadway, 2d floor
FOSTER, CHARLES, (Foster & Calkins) res n s Hubbard bet
Cherry and Chestnut
Foster Nathanial G, lumber mill 28 Cedar
FOSTER, CHARLES M flour and feed, res ne cor Hubbard and
Cherry
Fowles, Carlton, ship-carpenter, res Fowles' ship yard
Fowles, John, res Fowles' ship yard
Fowles, William, ship carpenter, res Fowles' ship yard
Franks, C, jeweler, res e s Broadway
Freeman, C, tug captain, res w s Sixth Avenue 2d s of G B & M
R R
Fredericksen, A, res s s Second st bet Fifth and Sixth Avenue
Frank, Kristien, res s s Elmore bet Broad and Chestnut
Fraikin, H, works in foundry, bds s s Fourth st 2d e Fourth
Avenue
Fraiken, J, works in foundry, res s s Fourth st 2d e Fourth Ave-
nue
Fuller, Mrs Catharine, wid res e s of Broadway 3d s of Hubbard
Fuller, David, laborer, res e s of Broadway 3d s of Hubbard
Fuller, Geo, laborer,bds e s of Broadway 3d s of Hubbard

G

Gain. John, carpenter, res w s Cherry bet Kellogg and Elmore
Garlock, B F, carpenter, res w s Willow, 3th s Elmore
Gaslin, J A, machinist, res Broadway
Gagnon, Prosper. restaurant keeper s s Main 1st w bridge, res
same
G B & M R R Depot 3d e Broadway, n s Third st
G B & M Freight Depot 2d e Broadway, s s Third st
Geelan, John, laborer e s Cherry, bet Main and Baird
Geiger, J, Brewer at Bay Brewery
Geisler, C, teamster, res n s Second st 3d e Fourth Avenue
Geisler, F, teamster. bds n s Second st 3d e Fourth Avenue
Gerka, E, works in furniture shop, bds ne cor Third st and Fourth
Avenue
Gelberson, Mena, servant Rev L H Duhl e s Chestnut below
Bond
Gerbsch, Herman, restaurant Salschridiers Block, res same
Gilbert, C, yard-master. bds sw cor Seventh Avenue and Third
street
Gilenbach, Katie, house keeper Seymour House
Gillis, Alex, sailor, res ne cor Dousman and Cedar
Glass, John foreman William Peck, res e s Cherry. bet Kellogg
and Elmore

Glostermann, Louis, carpenter, res e s Broadway
Gothier, Alex. carpenter, res on Mather w Willow
Goodman, William, cooper, res n s Main bet Cherry and Willow
Gort, John, wagon maker E Brehme, res cor Baird and Chestnut
Greiser, Gottlieb, laborer, res s s Elmore w Willow
Graves, Philo H, produce dealer, res e s Willow 1st n of Main
Graves, Frank, machinist res Green Bay
Graves, Joseph, carpenter C. Schwarz & Co, res Green Bay
Graves, O J, tin-smith, res s s Second st 2d w Fourth Avenue
Gray, William H, grocer s s of Main 3d w Broadway, res e s
    Chestnut bet Main and Hubbard
Gray, William, grocer, bds e s Chestnut 3d n Baptist Church
Gray, Oscar, lumberman, res w s Chestnut 4th s Hubbard
Gray, A L, capitalist, res e s Cedar 2d n Hubbard
Guesnier, A Jr, book keeper W G Bruce & Co res Green Bay
Guetzlaugh. J, laborer, res sw cor Fifth Avenue and Third st
Gunderson, Salva, Lake captain, res e s of Pearl 1st s of Monitor
    Iron Works
Gunsley, J. laborer, res e s Fifth Avenue, 3d s of Ninth st
Gust, — laborer, res n s Dousman 9th w Willow

H

Hackett, Michael, R R engineer, res n s Chestnut, bet Hub-
    bard and Dousman
Haffy, E J, painter, bds Hibenia House
Hagenson, H, wood sawyer, res n s Third st, 3d e Fifth Ave
Haight, W H, farmer, res Mather, w Willow
Haight, W H, bds Northwestern Hotel
Halgesen, J, laborer, res e s Fourth Ave, 2d s Seventh st
Hall House, Jos LeBel, proprietor, ne cor Broadway and
    Baird
Hallemer, Mrs D, wid, res with John Martin on Pearl
Hall, Sewrin, sailor, res w s Broadway, 1st s Baird
Hall, W A, (Hall & Burns,) Hardware, w s of Broadway, 3d
    n of Main, res Cherry st
Hammerstrom, Chas A, cabinet-maker, res n s Chestnut
Hansford, J, trader, res e s Fourth Avenue, 4th n Ninth st
Hanrahan, Patrick, carpenter, res e s Cedar, 4th n Main
Hanrahan, J M, carpenter, res e s Cedar, 4th n Main
Hanrahan, Michael, carpenter, res e s Cedar, 4th n Main
Hanson, M Hans, laborer, res w s Third Avenue, 1st s Ninth
Hanson, Martin, laborer, nw cor Broadway and Ninth st
Hanson, H, carpenter, C Schwarz & Co, bds n s Fifth st, 2d
    w Fourth Avenue
Hanson, Ole, carpenter, res n s Fourth st, 2d w Broadway
Hanson, Hans M, teamster, bds n s Fourth st, 2d w Broadway

Hanson, R V, proprietor Ashery, res w s Broadway, 1st s Fourth st
Hansen, Peter, bds Broadway House
Hanson, Mary, servant, res e s Sixth Avenue, 3d s G B & M R R,
Hanson, Annie, servant at Scandinavian House
Hanson, L, laborer, bds ne cor Fifth Avenue and First st
Hanson, L, sailor, res nw cor Fifth Avenue and Third st
Hanson, C, laborer, res se cor Fifth Avenue and Second st
Hansen, Mary, servant, n s Hubbard, bet Cherry & Chestnut
Hanneshan, Thos, blacksmith, G B & M R R, bds ne cor of Broadway and Second st
Hansen, A, (Hansen & Roger) proprietor of Union House, e s of Broadway, bet First and Second sts
Hansen, Ingen Maria, servant, Union House
Harnsen, Mattie S, servant at Union House
Hartman, Sylvester, saloon keeper, e s Pearl, 2d n John, res e s Pearl, 3d n John
Haunson, Mrs Elizabeth, wid, res w s Seventh Avenue, 3d n of school house
Hawley, Thomas, steamboat captain, res e s Chestnut, 2d n Main
Hayden, John, res s s Elmore, w Willow
Hea, W, laborer, bds sw cor Seventh Avenue and Third st
Hea, M, piano ag't. bds sw cor Seventh Avenue and Third st
Healy, Mary. dress-maker, res s s Elmore, 1st w Willow
Healy, Anna Miss, teacher, res s s Elmore, 1st w Willow
Healy, John, caulker and ship carpenter, res s s Elmore, 1st w Willow
Hebron, J, laborer, res e s Third Avenue, 2d s Seventh st
Heffren, C, boiler-maker, bds Ft Howard House
Heidberg , L, tinsmith, res s s Third st, 1st e Broadway
Heidgen, Matthias, blacksmith, e s Broadway, bet Main and Baird, res w s Cherry, bet Main and Baird
Helgenson, H R, carpenter, res ne cor Fourth Avenue and Eighth st
Helner, S E, ship carpenter, res nw cor Third Avenue and Eighth st
Henderson, D Mrs, wid, David, res s s Mather, 2d w Cherry
Henderson, James L. painter. res s s Mather, 2d w Cherry
Henderson, E F, painter, res s s Mather, 2d w Cherry
Henderson, R, paint shop. ne cor Hubbard and Broadway
Henderson, Rob't, painter, res w s Cherry, 2d s Main
Hendrickson, W H, laborer, res n s Chestnut, bet Kellogg and Elmore
Hensen, —, wid, seamstress, res s s Dousman, 8th w Willow

Hensen, Albert, laborer, res s s Dousman, 10th w Willow
Hibernia House, P S Shaughnessy, prop'r, e s Brodway, bet
　Kellogg and Elmore
Hickey, James, carpenter, res Mather, w Willow
Hickey, Martin, section boss, res e s Cedar, 6th n Main
Hilbert, E C, caulker, res n s Fourth st, 1st w Fourth Ave
Hogan, James, drayman, res s s Elmore, w Willow
Hogan, Matt, laborer, res n s Elmore, w Willow
Hogan, Patrick, drayman, res n s Elmore, w Willow
Hogan, Nora, servant, s s Second st, 2d w Fourth Avenue
Holb, James, sawyer, res ne cor Eighth Ave, and Third st
Holleran, Mary, servant, Cornucopia House
Hood, Wm, night-watchman, res se cor Baird and Cedar
Honigan, Mrs Annie, wid, res on Dousman st
Honigan, Miss Annie, compositor, Green Bay Advocate
Holst, John, carpenter, C Schwarz & Co, res w s Cherry,
　1st n Main
Howard, Adolph, blacksmith, bds e s Broadway, 4th s of
　Second st
Howard Foundry, Taylor & Duncan, prop'rs, Pearl, 1st n
　slough
Howland, A, carpenter, res sw cor Ninth Avenue and Sixth
HOWLAND, L, lumberman and dealer, res w s Sixth Avenue,
　1st s G B & M R R
Howlett, John, captain steamer, res s s Elmore, w Willow
Howlitt, Mary E. dress maker, bds sw cor Broadway and
　Eighth st
Howlitt, Jas, carpenter, res sw cor Broadway and Eighth st
Hubbard, Hiram, farmer, res Mather, w Willow
Hudson, P, laborer, res sw cor Fourth Avenue & Second st
Hudson, Samuel, mason, res Main, w Willow
Huffman House, E Lawler, proprietor, s s Hubbard, bet
　Broadway and Chestnut
Hummarstrom, Hilma, servant, ne cor Baird and Cherry
Humpriville, Wm, printer, Monitor office, res Cherry, bet
　Main and Hubbard
HUNT, DOMINICK, dry goods and groceries, sw cor Dous-
　man and Broadway, res same
Hunter, Miss Azalia, school teacher, bds e s Seventh Avenue,
　Second s First st
Hunt, Mrs Patrick, wid, res n s Bond, 4th w Willow
Hull, W C, blacksmith, res nw cor Bond and Baird
Hummerstrom, C A, cabinet-maker, res w s Chestnut below
　Bond
Hurley, Annie, servant, e s Broadway, 2d s of Clark

I

Ilra, Anton, meat-market, w s Broadway, 1st w postoffice
Illebeck, Emmuel, painter, res sw cor Broadway and Ninth st
Iverson, A M, Moravian Clergyman, res se cor Fourth Avenue and Fourth st
Iverson, A M, grocer, nw cor Broadway and Second st
Iverson, M, clerk Scand'n House

J

Jacobs, Stephen, bookkeeper Taylor & Duncan, res Green Bay
Jacobson. E, laborer, res e s Eighth Avenue, opposite park
Jacobson, Jacob, caulker, res s s Dousman, 7th w Willow
Jacobson, Andrew, carpenter, res e s Third s of Seventh
Jacobson, Anna, dressmaker, bds e s Third Avenue 3d s Seventh st
Jacobson, Amund, carpenter, res se cor Eighth st and Fourth Avenue
Jacobsdater, Mary, servant at Bay Brewery
Jackson, M, ship-carpenter, res sw cor Fourth Avenue and Eighth st
Jansen, Andrew, laborer, resides nw cor of Broadway and Third street
Jansen, Peter, blacksmith, bds, at Union House
Jansen Mrs, wid, res w s of Broadway, 2d n of Third st
Jansen, Martin, sailor, res nw cor of Third and Broadway
Jansen, Christoff, furnaceman, res nw cor Broad and Third st
Allen, James, bookkeeper N W Depot, bds Northwestern House
Jargenson, Ole, grocer, w s Broadway 1st n bridge, res same
Jarpin, Hugo, laborer, res w s Third Avenue, 3d s Seventh st
Jarpin, Wm, laborer, bds w s Third Avenue, 3d s Seventh st
Jarpin, W, drayman, bds w s Third Avenue, 3d s Seventh st
Janslin, J H, engineer, res w s Broadway bet Hubbard and Main
Jencks, S R, (Jencks & Clinton) res n s Hubbard bet Cherry and Chestnut
Jencks, Clifford, clerk Jenks & Clinton, res n s Hubbard bet Broadway and Chestnut
Jencks, Shepherd R, (Jencks & Clinton) res n s Hubbard bet Broadway and Chestnut
Jenkins, L F, carpenter, res n s Dousman 1st e Willow
Jensen, Mary res w s Cedar, 2d s Elmore
Jensen Harold. ship-carpenter, res e s Third Avenue 1st north Eighth st
Jensen, Sena, servant e s Broadway bank of Fox River bet Seventh and Eighth st

Jensen, D, wid, res w s Broadway 4th s Third st
Jewell, P. teamster, res se cor Third Avenue and Seventh st
Jenson, William, foreman Monitor Iron Works, res e s Willow bet Main and Baird
Johnson, T C, foreman Herald office, bds Fort Howard House
Johnson, Peter, furniture, res e s Chestnut
Johnson, M C, grocer n s of Main 3d e of Broadway, res same
Johnson, — res n s Elmore 1 w Willow
Johnson, John, ship-carpenter, res n s Dousman, 10th w Willow
Johnson, Andrew J, laborer, res 128 Main
Johnson, Bernard, cooper, Tanktown
Johnson, R J, butcher, w s of Broadway, 4th n of Third st
Johnson, Peter F, furniture s s Main bet Pearl and Broadway, res Pearl
Johnson, Henry, res n s Chestnut bet Kellogg and Elmore
Johnson, Lars, carpenter and joiner, bds s s Second st 2d e Fifth Avenue
Johnson, R, works on dock, bds s s Second st 3d w Fourth Avenue
Johnson, P T, laborer, res s s Second st 2d w Fourth Avenue
Johnson, M, bds se cor Fourth Avenue and Fourth st
Jones, P, laborer, res s s Third st 3d w Broadway
Jordan, Joseph, plasterer, res Mather w Willow
Jorgeson, Rasmus, laborer, res w s Broadway, 3d south Fifth st
Jorgenson, J, laborer, res ne cor Fourth Avenue and Eighth st
July, John. barkeeper Eagle saloon, res ne cor Broadway and Third st
July. Minnie, res ne cor of Broadway and Third st

K

KALMBACH M. F. wholesale fresh and salt fish, n s Main 1st w bridge, res w s Cherry 2d n Dousman
Keiser, H, laborer, residence s s Fifth st 2d w of Seventh Avenue
Kemintz, Richard, carpenter, res e s Broadway
Kemper, Chapel —— rector se cor Main and Chestnut
Keney, Patrick, brakesman C & N W R R, bds at Sherman House
Kennedy, Danl, switchman C & N W R R bds at Sherman House
Kemnetz, Theodore, (Schwarz & Co) res ne cor Main and Cedar
Keppler, Frank, compositor Herald office, bds at Mrs Jansen's Green Bay
Kerby, Lewis, carpenter, res Mather w Willow
Kerr, J, boiler-maker, res ne cor Seventh Avenue and Third st

Kerr, James, job printer State Gazette Green Bay, bds North-western House

Ketchum, Mrs, house keeper e s Chestnut 2d n Baptist Church

King, Mrs Rose, r s s Elmore bet Broadway and Chestnut

King, Louis, book keeper, res s s Elmore bet Broadway and Chestnut

Kinney, Martin, bds Broadway House

Kinsey, Jennie, servant ne cor Broadway and Second st

Klaassen, Henry, tailor, res w s Chestnut bet Main and Baird

Klaussen, J H, prop'r of Bakery, w s of Pearl, next n Sherman House, res with H Klaassen

Klingen, Mrs C, wid, res w s Pearl, 1st n Scand'n Hotel

Klostermann, L, turner, C Schwarz & Co, res e s Broadway, bet Baird and John

Knobson, Ole, prop'r saloon and Boarding House, e s Broadway foot of Fourth st

Knowles, Mary, wid, John, res e s Chestnut, bet Main & Baird

Knudsen, Elias, laborer, res e s Cherry, bet Main and Baird

Koch, Oscar, book keeper, res w s Cedar, 1st n Main

Koch, Oscar, grocer, res w s Broadway, 3d s Baird

Koch, Oscar, book keeper, res w s Broadway, 3d s Baird

Kripner, B, machinist, Howard Foundry, res s s Baird, bet Chestnut and Cherry

Krog, F, Mason, res w s Ninth Avenue, s of Park

Krog, H, mason, res w s Fifth Avenue, 2d s Third st

Krog, J, lab, res e s Seventh Avenue, 2d s of Third st

Krug, John, watchman, C Schwarz & Co, res Fourth Aveuue

Kuhl, J, milk-man, res s s Ninth st, 2d w Ninth Avenue

Kull, F J, engineer C Schwarz & Co, res n s Third st, 3d e Fourth Avenue

Kullenbach, M F, board of education Ft Howard

Kummerlein' C, works in elevator, res w s Broadway, 2d s Eighth

L

LeBel, J, carpenter, res s s Cedar, 2d n Dousman

LeBel, Joseph, prop'r Hall House, nw cor Broadway and Baird

LaBelle, Jos, saloon keeper, res main w Willow

LaCombe, Frank, laborer, bds Huffman House

LeComb, Alex, res n s Elmore, w Willow

LeComb, Alex Jr, drayman, res n s Bond w Willow

Ladd, F, machinist, Howard Foundry

Ladd, F, machinist, res nw cor Fifth Avenue and Second st

Laget, A, prop'r grocery store, nw cor Broadway & Fourth

Lahan, Michael, laborer, res n s Dousman, 3d w Willow

Laird, J, works in mill yard, bds n s Second st, 3d e Fifth Av

Laird, F, clerk in grocery store, bds n s Second st, 3d e
Fifth Avenue
LAIRD, J P, lumberman, res n s Second st, 3d e Fifth Ave
Lampson, C, lumberman. res w s Fourth Avenue, 1st s
Clinton & Lairds Mill
Lampson, Chas, (Laird & Co,) lumber manuf'r and dealer,
res Second st and Fourth Avenue
Lanagan, John, book-keeper, res n s Hubbard, bet Chestnut
and Cherry
Lanagan, Jos, machinist and engineer, bds n s Hubbard, bet
Chestnut and Cherry
Lanhard, Fred, engineer, G B & M R R, res e s of Broad-
way, 2d s of Second st
Lannay, Frank, res s s Elmore, 3d e Willow
Lannay, Jerry, res s s Elmore, 3d e Willow
Lannay, Fred, res s s Elmore, 3d w Willow
Lannay,, A, res s s Elmore, 3d w Willow
Lanstin, H, serv't, res w s Sixth Ave, 2d s of G B & M R R
Larrowel, J, carpenter, res ne cor Second st and Eighth Ave
Larson, C, carpenter, res n s Second st, 2d e Eighth Avenue
Larson. J, works on dock, bds s s Second st, 3d w Fourth Ave
Larson, Addie, serv't, bds e s Fifth Avenue, 1st n Ninth st
Larson, J, laborer, res e s Fifth Aaenue, 1st n Ninth st
Larson, A, tailor, res w s Broadway, Second s Fourth st
Larson, C, laborer, res es Fourth Avenue, 4th s Ninth st
Larson, Chris. laborer, res w s Third Avenue, 4th s Ninth st
Lavette, Chas, farmer, res Mather, w Willow
Law, Jerry, farmer, res Main, w Willow
Lawler, Mrs Isabel, dress maker, res n s Hubbard, bet Cedar
and Willow
Lawler, E, prop'r Huffman House, s s Hubbard, bet Broad-
way and Chestnut
Legot, Victor, moulder, res e s Cherry, 1st n Hubbard
LeMont, Joseph, res Mather, w Willow
Leonard, D, blacksmith, res ne cor Sixth Ave and Third st
Lett, Wm H, lumber merchant, res e s Broadway 2d s Baird
Levy, Mandle, merchant, s s Main, bet Pearl and Broadway,
res se cor Willow and Hubbard
Lewins, Rob't brickmaker, res e s Cedar, 4th n Dousman
Lightbody, S, machinist, bds sw cor Seventh Avenue and
Third st
Lilly, Henry, clerk, n s of Main, 2d e of Broadway
Linehan, R, carpenter, res se cor Main and Cherry
Lochart Nicholas, bds Broadway House
Lochart, Wm, bds Broadway House
Lohrei, Bertha, serv't, e s Willow, bet Main and Baird

Lohrey, Emily, serv't, res e s Broadway, 3d s Third st

Lonzo, Jos, barber, basement se cor Main and Pearl, res es Cedar, bet Main and Hubbard

LeBel, Libbie, res e s Cedar, 2d n Dousman

Lucas, A, printer, res n s Hubbard, bet Cedar and Willow

Lucas, F, shingle maker, res n s Dousman, 3d w Willow

Lucas, A, city marshal, res e s Willow, 4th s Dousman

Lucas, Dan, tinsmith, res Main, w Willow

Luckey, Caroline, wid, T H, res s s Hubbard, 1st e Willow

Luckey, Chas F, breakman, res s s Hubbard, 1st e Willow

Ludd, Oscar, bds Broadway House

Ludlke, A, blacksmith, res w s Fifth Ave, 1st s Ninth st

Lund, E, mason, res sw cor Eighth Avenue, and First st

Lyhene, P, section man, res e s Cherry, 3d s Hubbard

Lyons, Chas, commercial traveler, bds n s Kellogg bet Chest-nut and Broadway

Lyons, J, accountant, res nw cor Fourth Avenue and Third st, opp Congregational Church

M

Maas, W, turner, C Schwarz & Co, res Green Bay

Maloney, Wm, prop'r of saloon and boarding honse, w s of Pearl, 7th n of Main, res same

Maloney, Jas, laborer, res nw cor Cherry and Kellogg

Manning, John, machinist, res e s Willow bet Main & Baird

Marcne, John, hired man, e s broadway, 1st s Ninth st

Marcues, John, clerk, Mandle Levy, bds se cor Willow and Hubbard

Market, Wm, butcher, L Nelson & Co, bds Whitney House

Mars, Julius, merchant, e s Broadway, 3d s Second st, res next south

Marshall, F S, cl'k T M Camm, res n s Hubbard, bet Cherry and Cedar

Marshall, Wm Mrs, milliner, s s Main, 3d w Broadway, res e s Chestnut, bet Main and Hubbard

Marshall, Linas L, shingle merchant, res sw cor Dousman and Chestnut

Marshall, Wm, lab, res e s Chestnut, 3d n Baptist Church

Martin, John, prop'r of saloon, w s Pearl, 8th e Main, r same

Mason, Jos, saloon keeper, s s Main, 4th w bridge, res opp Huffman House

Mason, S, carriage-maker, bds at Montreal House

Matteson, C, lab, res e s Fourth Avenue, 3d n Ninth st

Maumble, Moses, foreman and blacksmith, res s s Baird, 1st w Pearl

Maynerd, M P, carpenter, res Mather, w Willow

Maymbl, Jos, blacksmith, res s s Baird, bet, Broadway and Main
McArther, J, blacksmith, res e s Fifth Ave, 4th s Ninth st
McCabe, Owen, clerk, Cornucopia House
McCann, M F, bds Broadway House
McCARTNEY, DAVID, dealer in lumber, e s Broadway, 2d s Dousman, res nw cor Main and Cherry
McCay, Mary, res e s Pearl, bet Main and Hubbard
McCormick, P, laborer, res e s Willow, 2d n Main
McCormick, M, book-keeper, Monitor Iron Works res G B
McCormick, Jas, prop'r Forest City House
McCulley, Kate, serv't, Cornucopia House
McDonnell, Jas, architect, res nw cor Baird and Cherry
McDonnell, J H, student, res nw cor Baird and Cherry
McDonald, Denis, lab, res se cor Cherry and Hubbard
McQuade, Ella, serv't, s s Main, 1st w bridge
McNamara, John, bds Broadway House
Mechanics Exchange, ——, prop'r, w s Broadway, bet Dousman and Kellogg
Merchant, Oliver, (Merchant & Co,) prop'r Ft Howard saloon, w s Pearl, n Main, bds at Huffman House
Mercy, Nelson, lab, res e s Broadway. 2d s Hubbard
Mellville, M, engineer, bds Ft Howard House
Miller, F, lab, res e s Cedar, 1st s Baird
Miller, Wm, moulder, res e s Cedar, 1st s Baird
Miller, M, stationary eng, res ne cor Broadway and Third st
Miller, Michael, laborer, res e s Cedar, 2d n Hubbard
Miney, Bridget, serv't, w s Broadway, bet Bond and Mather
Moeller, A, wagon maker, E Breheme, bds w s Broadway, 2d s Main
Molither, Minnie, serv't, w s Chestnut, 2d n Main
Montreal House, e s of Pearl, bet Main and Hubbard, P Saloo, prop'r
Monitor Iron Works Co, e s Pearl, 5th s Main
Mooney, Thos, bds Broadway House
Moravian Church, se cor Fifth Avenue and Fourth st
Morrell, N, (Morrell & Co,) flour and feed, whol, w s Broadway, bet Main and Baird, res e s Broadway
Morgan, E B, (Morgan & Cobb,) gas fitter, e s Pearl, 5th n Main, res Ft Howard
Morganson, H, lab, bds se cor Fifth Ave, and Second st
Morningston, Rufus, tinsmith, bds s s Main, 1st w bridge
Mountain, A, prop'r Dousman House, se cor Broadway and Dousman
Moveran. Sophia, serv't, res se cor Fourth Ave, & Fourth st
Mulligahn, Michael, bds Broadway House

Mullin, Michael, laborer, se cor Bond and Cedar
Mulqueen, B, wid, James, res w s Cherry, 4th s Hubbard
Munson, Ale, watch-maker, res s s Second s 3d w Fourth Ave
Murphy, Ellen, servant, nw cor Broadway and Ninth st
Murphy, J, machinist, Howard Foundry, bds Ft Howard
House
Murphy, J L, machinist, bds Ft Howard House
Murphy, P, prop'r of Home saloon, sw cor Broadway and
Second st, res same
Murphy, Wm, laborer, n s Bond, 1st w Broadway
Murray, J, fireman R R, res nw cor Sixth Ave & Second st
Murtz, Conrad, watchman, res w s Cedar, 3d n Main

N

NANSCAWEN, CALEB, (Nanscawen & Son,) physician. res
115 Main
NANSCAWEN, JOSHUA, (Nanscawen & Son, druggist, res
115 Main
Neehtges, John, teamster, bds Sherman House
Neilson, Geo, lab, res s s Fourth st, next Moravian Church
Neilson, Mary C, wid, res w s Fifth Avenue, 1st n Fifth st
Neilson, A, sailor, res e s Broadway, 1st n Fifth st
Neilson, A, sailor, bds ne cor Fourth Avenue and Fifth st
Neilson, L, lab, res s s Second st, 3d e Fourth Avenue
Neilson, P, res ne cor Fourth Avenue and Fifth st
Neilson, J, sailor, res ne cor Fourth Avenue and Fifth st
Neilson, H, carpenter, res n s Fifth st, 2d e Fourth Avenue
Neilson, O, lab, res e s Fourth Avenue, 3d s Ninth st
Neilson, J, teamster, bds s s Second st, 2d w Fourth Avenue
Nelson, A, teamster, bds at Scandinavian House
Nelson, Andrew, carpenter, res e s Pearl, 2d s Monitor Iron
Works
Nelson, D, laborer, bds at Scandinavian House
Nelson, L, (L Nelson & Co,) res s s Main, 2d w Broadway
Neuman, L, confectionary and fruits, n s Main, 2d w bridge,
res w s Cedar, bet Main and Hubbard
Neville, Sarah J, servant, sw cor Mather and Cherry
NEWALD, M, clothing, res nw cor Cherry and Baird
Newald, M Jr, clerk, nw cor Main and Pearl
New London House, se cor Broadway
Newland, N, Mason, res e s Broadway, 2d s Third st
Normann, Lazerus, merchant, res w s Cedar, 2d n Main
Norman, John G, painter, res e s Cedar, 5th n Main
Novelty Iron Works, w s Pearl, cor Baird
N W R R Passenger Depot, Pearl, s of slough
N W R R Freight Depot, se cor Broadway and Elmore
Nye, Geo, carpenter, bds Cornucopia House

O

O'Connel, Michael, bds Broadway House
O'Leary, M, boiler maker, res Green Bay
O'Leary, H, boiler maker, res Green Bay
O'Leary, T, boiler maker, res Green Bay
O'Leary, Humphry, prop'r Boiler Works, w s Pearl, 1st s
    Main, res Green Bay
O'Leary, Daniel, boiler maker, res Green Bay
O'Leary, John, boiler maker, res Green Bay
Oldenberg, G, furniture dealer, res ne cor Fourth Avenue
    and Third st
Oldenberg, A, works in furniture shop, bds ne cor Fourth
    Avenue and Third st
Oleson, Mary, wid, res e s Fourth Avenue, 2d s Ninth st
Oleson, Jacob, lab, res w s Third Avenue, 2d s Ninth st
Oleson, A, lab, res w s Broadway, 2d s Ninth st
Oleson, W, moulder, res s s First st, 2d w Fifth Avenue
Oleson, H, plasterer, res s s Fourth st, 1st w Broadway
Olesen, W, moulder, res opp Howard Foundry
Olesen, Wm, moulder, Howard Foundry. res Tank Town
Olesen, L, ship carpenter, res w s Broadway, 4th s Baird
Olsen, B, sailor, res Main. w Willow
Olsen, A B, clerk, n s Main, e Broadway, res Broadway
Olsen, O, shoemaker, bds Scandinavian House
Olsen, A B, clerk. res w s Broadway, bet Hubbard and Main
Olsen, Ole, laborer, res e s Cherry, bet Main and Baird
Olson, O L, carpenter, bds Northwestern House
O'Neil, P, foreman C & N W R R, res e s Broadway. 3d s
    Third st
Orbit, —, cooper, res Main, w Willow
Oul, Geo, watchman, Howard Foundry, res sw cor Pearl
Owens, Geo, engineer, res e s Broadway, bet Baird and ——
Owen, A, res e s Broadway, bet Baird and ——

P

Paulsen, P, lab, res w s Broadway, 4th s Ninth st
Peak, W H, res e end Main
Peak, H W, brakeman, L P R R. res e s Willow, 2d s
    Dousman
Peiper, Wm, machinist, Howard Foundry, bds e s main, bet
    Dousman and Chestnut
Pennissen, J, teamster, res s s Fourth st, 3d e Fourth Ave
Penrad, Erwin, laborer, res w s Cedar, 3d s Elmore
Penrad, Geo H, laborer, res e s Cedar, 3d s Elmore
Perrigoue, W, laborer. res Main, w Willow

Perry, G, clerk in grocery store, bds s s First st, 1st e of
Fifth Averue
Perry, Geo W, moulder, res s s Eirst st, 1st e Fifth Avenue
Peterson, J C, clerk, A Ielra, res cor John and Chestnut
Peterson, Thos, blacksmith, res s s Dousman, 6th e Willow
Peterson, C, laborer, res s s Third st, 3d w Broadway
Peterson, N, laborer, bds s s Second st, 2d w Fourth Avenue
Peterson, P O, moulder, res s s Second st, 3d w Fourth Ave
Peterson, Hannah, servant, sw cor Main and Cherry
Peterson, H, carpenter, res ne cor Seventh Ave & Second st
Peterson, Chas, butcher, bds s s John, 2d w Broadway
Peterson, Orlena, servant, e s Broadway, 4th s Second st
Peterson, Alex P, mason, res w s Cherry, s Baird
Petersen, Lena, servant, nw cor Main and Cherry
Petersen, L, section man, res e s Cherry, 1st s Main
Petersen, Wm H, clerk, res w s Chestnut, s Baird
Petersen, Thos, blacksmith, e s Broadway, 3d s Baird
Petersen, N B, clerk, res w s Cherry, 2d s Baird
Pfister, Rob't, carpenter, C Schwarz & Co, bds e s Broad-
way, bet Baird and John
Phelts, H, barber, J Lonzo, res cor Main and Pearl, bds
Northwestern House
Phillips, Henry, barber, bds Northwestern House
Philbrook, Richard, laborer, res n s Cherry, s Baird
Pinto, A N, commercial traveller, M F, Kalmbach, res G B
Crooks st
Planert, Frantz, boots and shoes, retail, s s Main, 2d w bridge,
res Coopers town
Planert, A, foreman, F Planert, res s s Main, 2d w bridge
Plank, Nelson, G, res w s Pearl, 3d n John
Platten, J, prop'r Wis House, w s Pearl, bet Main & Hubbard
Plunen, T, foundryman, res w s Chestnut, s Baird
Plaws, W Prof, of music, bds sw cor Seventh Ave & Third st
Poitras, Nelson, cooper, res Mather, w Willow
Pollan, M, laborer, bds at Montreal House
Poole, M L, eng, R R, res e s Seventh Avenue, 2d s of First
Powers, Thos, carpenter, res e s Willow, bet Main and Baird
Preston, Sam, livery stable, e s Broadway, bet Main and
Baird, res w s Cedar
Prevat, Dorcas, serv't, n s Main, 3d e of Broadway
Purner, C H, book keeper, J A Salscheider, res Baird
Pym, Geo, laborer, res e s Willow 3d n Main
Pym, Wm, laborer, res e s Willow, 3d n Main

Q

Quade, Patrick, lahorer, res e s Broadway, 2d n Depot

R

Ralph, Geo D, machinist, res s s John, 2d w Broadway
Ralph, H M Mrs, wid, O H, res s s John, 2d w Broadway
Rasmaulen, P J, clerk, W G Bruce & Co, res Green Bay
Rasmussen, A, laborer, res se cor Seventh Ave and First st
Rasmussen, E, res w s Fourth Avenue, 2d n Ninth st
Redline, Ed, baggage man, G B & M R R, bds ne cor of
  Broadway and Third st
Remington, John, laborer, bds opp Huffman House
Reinhardt, C, laborer, res n s Fourth st, 2d e Fifth Avenue
Reischenbach, P, wagon maker, bds w s Cherry, bet Main
  and Baird
Reynolds, H, street commissioner, res Main w Willow
Rice, A, carpenter, res e s Fourth Avenue, 3d s Seventh st
Rice, Dan, laborer, res e s Broadway, 1st n Hubbard
Rice, H M, carpenter, bds Ft Howard House
Rice, H M, blacksmith, bds sw cor Seventh Avenue and
  Third st
Richardson, Geo, wood and tie ag't, L P R R, res w s Broad-
  way, bet Bond and Mather
Rich, Hans, gardner, res n s Dousman, 6th e Willow
Rickter, C C, tailor, res se cor Third st and Fourth Avenue
Riley, Jos, brakeman, C & N W R R, res Sherman House
Riley, T, prop'r Sherman House
Ritter, Wm, brewer at Bay Brewer
Roager, C, (Hansen & Roager,) prop'r Union House
Robinson, Yankee Nathan, Peddlar, bds Wis House
Rockett, Mrs M, wid, res sw cor Third Ave and Eighth st
Rodhe, B, blacksmith, E Brehme, bds w s Broadway, 2d s
  Main
Rohan, J, brakeman, C & N W R R, bds Sherman House
Roice, Geo W, R R conductor, res se cor Dousman and Chest-
  nut sts
Rose, Henry, laborer, res s s Elmore, w Willow
Roskamps, Felix, saloon keeper, e s Cedar, bet Dousman and
  Elmore
Roskamps, Peter, res e s Cedar, bet Dousman and Elmore
Rood, Minnie, servant, Ft Howard House
Rossiter, M Mrs, wid John, res w s Pearl, bet Baird and——
Rossiter, Maria, 1st assistant teacher, public school 2d Ward,
  res w s Pearl, bet Baird and——
Rouser, F, lab, res w s Third Avenue, 2d s Eighth st
Rourk, John, laborer, res n s Dousman, 5th w Willow
Rutherford, B, machinist, res nw cor Hubbard and Cedar
Ryan, Patrick, teamster, res e s Cedar, 2d n Dousman

S

Sahlman. Olof, tailor, bds w s Broadway bet Main and Hub
bard
Saunders, J. laborer, res e s Broadway, 2d n Fifth st
Saxton, L, pattern maker Monitor Iron Works, res Tanktown
Salchrider, J A, saloon keeper Main nw cor Pearl, res same
Saloman, John, carpenter, res s s Hubl ard 1st e Cherry
Salvo, P, propr Montreal House
Saxton, L J, millwright, res ne cor Sixth Avenue and First st
Scambal, James, moulder. res w s Eighth Avenue se of Second st
Scandinavia Hotel, w s of Pearl, n of Main, J A Blichfeldt propr
Schafer, John, laborer C. Schwarz & Co, res South street
Schafer, C, se cor Ninth Avenue and Ninth st
Schettler, Frank, laborer, res w s Seventh Avenue, 2d n of school
house
Schettler. L, laborer, res sw cor Seventh Avenue and Fifth st
Schmidt, William, carpenter C Schwarz & Co. res Green Bay
Schmitz, Henry, truss maker e s Broadway 3d n Hubbard
Schneider, Anton, res e s of Broadway 5th s of Hubbard
Scholton, Rudolph, laborer. res nw cor Mather and Chestnut
Schulder, J, ship-carpenter, res s s Third st, 2d e Fifth Avenue
Schultz, P, farmer, res s s Second st 2d e Fifth Avenue
Scutte, Henry, bookkeeper C Schwarz & Co, res Green Bay
Schwarz, C, (Schwarze & Co) res w s Broadway bet Baird and
John sts
Schwarz, Oscar, bookkeeper, res nw cor Broadway and John
Seigman, W, carpenter, res s s Fourth st w Fourth Avenue
Seigmund, A, carpenter C Schwarz & Co, res Green Bay
Seigmond, H, carpenter, Schwarz & Co, res w s Broadway bet
Baird and John
Seigmund, Augusta, servant w s Broadway 4th s Baird
Seigrist. Adam, Prov and feed w s Broadway bet Main and Baird
Seim, W, laborer, bds w s Fifth Avenue 2d s G B & M R R
Seim, C, sailor, bds w s Fifth Avenue, 2d s G B & M R R
Seim, P, carpenter, bds w s Fifth Avenue, 2d s G B & M R R
Seim, Paul, laborer, res w s Fifth Avenue, 2d s G B & M R R
Sellers, Malcolm & Son commission merchants, res w s Broadway
3d s seventh st
Sellers, John, butcher s s Mather 3d w Cherry
Senigman, G blacksmith. res w s Fifth Avenue 2d n Third st
Sensiba, Mrs Elizabeth, laundry, res n s Baird bet Pearl and
Broadway
Sensiba, Erastus, shingle packer, res n s Baird bet Broadway and
Pearl
Sensiba, Albert, teamster, res n s Baird bet Broadway and Pearl

Servais, Peter, boots and shoes, s s of Hubbard, bet Broadway and Pearl

Servais, P J, compositor Herald office, res Hubbard

Shafer, Louis, farmer, res e s Broadway, 1st 9th st

Shanon, H, bar-keeper Hoffman House, s s Hubbard bet Broadway and Chestnut

Sharp. J. moulder, res se cor of Seventh Avenue and Third st

Sharly, J, laborer, res nw cor Fourth Avenue and Ninth st

Shaughnessy, J, servant, res ne cor Sixth Avenue and Third st

Shaughnessy, Patrick S, propr Hibernia House e s Broadway bet Kellogg and Elmore

Sheare, Henry, sawyer, bds Fort Howard House

Sheehy, Ed W, bds Broadway House

Sheridan, Peter, engineer steamer Fort Howard No 1, res n s Pearl, bet Main and Baird

Sherman House, w s of Pearl bet Main and Hubbard, T Riley propr
    res se cor Broadway and Hubbard

Simon, J, carpenter, res se cor Fifth Avenue and Ninth st

Simons, Antoine, propr Seymour House s s Maine 3d w bridge

Simmons, Alice, wid of Peter, res w s Cedar 3d n Main

Simmons, J, blacksmith, res w s Fifth Avenue 3d n of Second st

Skelley, James, laborer, bds e s Cherry bet Main and Baird

Slater, John, farmer, res Cornucopia House

Smith, P F, Engineer, bds sw cor Seventh Avenue and Third st

Smith, A H, broom factory, bds sw cor Seventh Avenue and Third st

Smith, Michael B, res Mather w Willow

Smith, Geo J, moulder, res e s Cedar bet Kellogg and Elmore

Smith, Geo B, teamster, res e s Cherry bet Elmore and Kellogg

Smith, Frank, bookkeeper Northwestern Hotel

Smith, B J, pattern maker, res w s Broadway 1st s Seventh st

Smith, Katy, school teacher, bds w s Broadway 1st s Seventh st

Smith, Mary E, dress maker, bds w s Broadway 1st s Seventh st

Smith, Freeman, laborer, res e s Fifth Avenue 1st s G B & M R R

Smith, David, clerk, bds s s Elmore bet Broadway and Chestnut

Smith, Wilson, machinist, res e s Cherry bet Main and Baird

Smith, Ernst, res w s Cedar 1st n Main

Smith, John, teamster, bds w s Cedar 1st n Main

Solbery, Halmer, teamster, res n s Main bet Cherry and Willow

Solbery, Peter, teamster. res n s Main bet Cedar and Willow

Sorenna, F, stone mason, res se cor Sixth Avenue and Third st

Sorenson, Elick, laborer, res e s Fourth Avenue 4th s Ninth st

Sorenson, J S, propr grocery store se cor 3d Avenue and Ninth street

SPENCE, ANDREW, grocer se cor of Broadway and Second s,t res same

Spence, nurseryman n s Second st 1 mile w Broadway

Sp⸱nce, Miss Elizabeth, keeps select school w s Seventh Avenue 2d s Third st

Spicer, Tom E, news dealer P O block, res s s of Main

Spier, Geo N, saloon Main n of Willow

Stearn, David, mason, res e s Cherry 1st s Dousman

Stevens, Theodore lumberman. res s s Elmore w Willow

Stinegar, A, laborer, res ne cor Fourth Avenue and Ninth st

Straight, Mrs Margaret, wid, res e s of Pearl, 6th n of Main

Strickanbau, Edward, shoe maker F Planert, res Green Bay

Sulivan, Mary, wid of Jerry, res se cor Cherry and Hubbard

Sulvo, John, lumberman street com, res opposite Huffman House

Summerfield, R, machinist, bds sw cor Seventh Avenue and Third st

Suquet, Constance, cooper, res e s Cherry 2d south Dousman

Sustman. F. Engineer in foundry, res s s Second st 2d e Fourth Avenue

Sustman, S, fireman Monitor Iron Works

Swetter, Frank, laborer, res s s Elmore w Willow

T

Tank, Mrs C D A, wid, res e s Broadway on bank of Fox River, bet Seventh and Eighth st

Tanner, John J, carpenter, res e s of Pearl 6th n of Main

Taylor, Wm H machinist, res e s Chestnut

Taylor, Jas, laborer. res Main w Willow

TAYLOR, JOSEPH, post master, res sw cor Broadway and John

Taylor, William S, (Ft Howard Foundry and Machine Works) res sw cor Main and Cherry

Taylor. Abraham, steam mill, res sw cor Cedar and Mather.

TAYLOR, R B, propr Taylor's patent shingle packer, bds Whitney House

Third Ward School. nw cor Seventh Avenue and Fifth st

Thompson. L, shoemaker, bds w s Broadway 4th s Third st

Thompson, Benjamin, boiler maker Fort Howard Boiler Works, res Green Bay

Thompson, Annie, servant, res sw cor Broadway and Third st

Thompson, S, carpenter, res n s Fourth st 2d e Fourth Avenue

Thompson, Jas, moulder Howard Foundry

Thompson, Wm Y, cooper, res n s Chestnut s Baird

Thompson, Mrs Annie, wid, res e s Sixth Avenue 2d s of G B & M R R

Thompson, John, ship-carpenter, res 63 Main

Thovison, Bertha, servant, res w s Broadway 3d s Third st

Tiernan, James, propr Fort Howard House
Tingloff, H, road master, res n s Fourth st 2d e Fourth Avenue
Tingloff, J, teamster, bds n s Fourth st 2d e Fourth Avenue
Tracy, James, cutter, res w s Broadway bet Main and Hubbard
Tuttle, W, carpenter, bds Cornucopia House

V

Van Berg, Miss, res n s Main 3d e Willow
Vanderberg, A, laborer, res s e cor Fifth st and Fifth Avenue
Vanderbrook, Peter, teamster, s s Elmore bet Chestnut and
  Cherry
Vanderbrook, William, mail carrier, res e s Broadway 1st n De-
  pot
Vanderboom, J, carpenter, res sw cor Fifth Avenue and Second
  street
Vaney, Leander, res e s Broadway 3d n Hubbard
Van Horn, C W, bookkeeper, res e s Sixth Avenue 3d s of G B
  & M R R
Vaughan, S, ship-builder, res w s Broadway 3d s of Third st
Viles, P, Brewer at Bay Brewery
View, Felix, carpenter, res Mather w Willow
Voigt, J, (Schwarz & Co) res n s Broadway, 8th s Baird

W

Walch, Frank, fisherman, res Fowles's shipyard
Walters, W, shoemaker, res se cor Second st and Eighth Ave
Walters, C H, train baggageman, res e s Cedar, 1st n Main
Walters, J, saloon keeper, e s Cedar, bet Dousman & Elmore
Wallenfang, Henry, shoemaker, n s Hubbard nr Pearl
Warren, O M, ag't Goodrich Transportation Co, res G Bay
Warren, Irvin, carpenter, res sw cor Broadway and Third st
Webster, G A, mail ag't, N W R R, w s Broadway, 2d s
  Mather
Welch, Patrick, bds Broadway House
Westmon, Mrs, wid, res nw cor Fourth Avenue and Fifth st
Whelen, D C, lumber, dealer, res ne cor Hubbard and Cedar
White, A, teamster, res e s Willow, 2d s Dousman
Whitmore, Mrs C, wid, res ne cor Fourth Ave & Second st
Whitney. Jonathan, foundryman, res 75 Main
Whilkaska, Lizzie, serv't, sw cor Seventh Ave & Third st
Williams, Jacob, lab, Kellogg & Elmore, res n s Chestnut
Williams, Henry, blacksmith, Thos Peterson, res Tank Town
Williams, J, machine ag't, bds sw cor Seventh Ave & Third st
Williams, W H, grocer, res ne cor Cedar and Baird
Williams. W H Mrs, music teacher, res ne cor Baird & Cedar
Williams W W, brakesman. G B & M R R bds at Sherman
  House

Williamson, Hannah, serv't, w s Chestnut, bet Dousman and Kellogg

Williamson, A, blacksmith, bds s s Fourth st, 1st w Broadway

Wilson, Wm, foreman, Monitor Iron Works

Wilson, Henry, laborer, res w s Broadway, 2d s Seventh st

Wilson, Wm, butcher, res Mather, w Willow

Winterbottom, J, machinist, res s s John, 2d w Broadway

Wirtz, Aug, lab, C Schwarz & Co, res e s Tenth Avenue, – s Park

WISCONSIN HOUSE, w s Pearl, bet Main and Hubbard

Wise, M, barber, bds Ft Howard House

Wittenger, J, ship-carpenter, res nw cor Ninth st & Third Av

Witters, Louis, mason, res w s Cedar, 1st s Elmore

Witters, O C, carpenter, res w s Chestnut, 2d s Hubbard

Wolfrath, F, clothier, w s Pearl, 3d e Main, res same

Wood, C, R R man. bds e s Chestnut, 2d n ——

Woodard, H K, carpenter, res w s Fifth Avenue, bet Fifth and Sixth sts

Woodward, J C, conductor, on G B & M R R, res sw cor Broadway and Third st

Woodward, Jas, carpenter, w s Cherry, bet Dousman and Kellogg

Wright, Geo B, dock master, res sw cor Cherry and Mather

Wright, ——, brakeman, N W R R. bds Northwestern Hotel

Y

Yates, Jane, wid, Francis, res w s Cherry, 2d s Hubbard

Z

Zenishek, J, moulder, res nw cor Third Ave and Ninth st

Zeigmund, Erwin, carpenter, O Schwarz & Co, res w s Broadway, bet Baird and John

Zizksowski, M, carpenter, C Schwarz & Co, res Green Bay

Zim, Wm, shoemaker, Frantz Planert, res Green Bay

TOWN OF PREBLE.

Beibel, Frank, teamster, res Grove st

Busch, A J, res n s Cedar

Cofman, Gottlieb, butcher, res cor Pleasant and Elm

Cofman, Louis, butcher, res cor Pleasant and Elm

Crone, Mrs Mary, wid, res Morrow, 3d n of Main

Crone, Jos, carpenter, res Morrow, 3d n of Main

Crone, Miss S, dress-maker, res Morrow, 3d n of Main

Charwork, Wenzel, blacksmith, res nw cor Cedar and Grove

Duken, Wenzel, tailor. res n s Cedar

Echen, John, laborer, res n s Cedar

Elmer, Chas L, lab, res Main, 2d n of Lumber yard

Felthaus, John, laborer, res Elm
Grimm, Wm, laborer, res foot of Cedar
Grimm, Joseph, laborer, res 1st e of terminus of Cedar
Graves, C, laborer in lumber yard. res n s Cedar
Graves, O B, attorney, res Morrow, 1st n of Main
Gonce, Wm, laborer, res st n of Willow
Hazleton, B F. book-keeper for J W Woodruff & Co. res
  Main, 1st n of lumber yard
Hogan, John, carpenter, res Cedar
Jaan, Emil, butcher, res e s Cedar, 1st w of Pleasant
Johnson, Geo. brickmaker, res terminus of Morrow
Langfurst, Wm, gardner, res n s Cedar, 1st w of Grave
Rapplye, H G, machinist. res Morrow. 2d n of Main
Schepek, John, tailor, res s s Elm, 3d e of Pleasant
Schleis, Jos, tanner, res s s Elm, 2d e of Pleasant
Shutte, H, saloon keeper. res foot of Elm
Smith, John M, gardner, res Morrow, 2d n of Main
Smith, F B, gardner, res Morrow, 3d n of Main
Triels, carpenter, res Main
Verboomen, Michael, saloon keeper, res cor Main and Cedar
Williams, Jos, laborer, res n s of Elm
Woodruff, J W & Co, lumber merchants, office 526 Main
Woodruff, J W, lumber merchant, res 525 Main
Woodruff, H E, lumber merchant, res 525 Main
Woodruff, W H, lumber merchant, res 525 Main

www.ingramcontent.com/pod-product-compliance
Lightning Source LLC
Chambersburg PA
CBHW020537270326
41927CB00006B/624